KV-405-327

# Contents

# Table

# Photographs

# Acknowledgments

I have often used the analogy of mountain climbing to describe the journey that I have undertaken in the writing of this dissertation. It required an intense spiritual and physical endurance to keep climbing. But I have been most fortunate to have had three mentors whom I greatly esteem:

Professor Burnham challenged me to search, find and apply the unique computer based technologies that would be the necessary tools for this journey.

Professor Astuto was the inspiration for this study. Her insight and compassion opened new understandings on the value of women's life experiences. In my moments of greatest anguish, she encouraged me to continue on.

Professor Rust provided a logical clarity to this study. Her valued advice was always most appreciated.

I wish to thank the nine women of the computer generations who participated in this study. They joyously shared their time to celebrate the truth: that professional women in education enjoy using computer based technologies.

Finally, I acknowledge my mother, who is no longer here, but whose life is still speaking of her sacrificial love. My pastor who lived the liberated life for almost a century and inspired us all. And my father whose dream has now come true.

# Chapter I

# Introduction and Problem Statement

## *The Problem Statement*

Quantitative research studies focusing on computer attitude, aptitude, and use in a variety of age groups in many countries suggest that there are gender-based differences that explain why women exhibit lower levels of computer use. For example, Shashaani (1992) found that there are differences in attitude (interest, confidence and stereotyping) toward computers among high school girls and boys that are significant and reflect gender-role socialization. Okebukola's research (1993) indicated that girls recorded a higher mean perceived anxiety about computer use than boys, who had a significantly higher mean score in computer interest. Makrakis's study (1992) of computer self-efficacy and equality in computer competence found significant gender differences in computer usefulness and prior computer experience acquired at school, both in favor of males.

However, other studies have found few if any gender differences in computer aptitude, attitude, and use. These studies reveal that there are fewer differences in computer aptitude, attitude, and use among preschoolers and primary grade students than among middle, secondary, and university students, which suggests that as male and female students grow older, more disparities emerge (Webb, 1994; Kay, 1992b; McGrath, Thurston, McLellan, Stone and Tischhauser, 1992).

Moreover, the contradictory results of research studies on attitude, defined in at least 14 different ways, suggest that there are no significant differences between men's and women's attitudes towards computers (Reinen and Plomp, 1993; Kay, 1992; Ogletree and Williams, 1990, etc.). Also, other research findings indicate that women have demonstrated superiority over men in computer adaptation (Vernon-Gerstenfeld, 1989) and computer problem-solving (Anderson, 1987). Why then, do these opposing research findings coexist? Is there a "conspiracy of silence" (Shakeshaft, 1987) concerning the competencies of women who use computers, work with tools and machines, and are world-renowned scientists and mathematicians? Is there an androcentric bias that pervades and perpetuates the myth of male dominance in a society that proclaims gender equity?

Harding (1991) explores the scientific basis of androcentrism in feminist epistemology. Harding proposes that society assumes that the concepts of women and knowledge—socially legitimated knowledge—have been constructed in opposition to each other. Therefore empirical scientific evidence is dismissed if it does not conform to the androcentric view of science in which the experiences of women are depreciated and neglected. Scientific research and evidence accepted for knowledge claims in our society must be reflected through the male voice and viewed from the male lens. Scientific research and evidence about computer based technologies have been well chronicled about men.

The purpose of this researcher is to investigate the use of computer based technologies by professional women in education through the lens of a theoretical framework that is sensitive to the unique experiences of women.

## Computer Based Technologies

Women's experiences with computer based technologies will be categorized using three levels: beginning, intermediate and advanced. These are not hierarchical classifications but refer to the range of experience across five types of computer applications. These are broad classifications derived from the 20 specific computer experiences charted in the Bank Street National Survey on Telecommunications (Honey & Henriquez, 1993). These types of computer experiences include: Experience with computer applications for drill and practice, educational games, etc.; experience with computer applications that involves learning with computers and keyboarding skills for wordprocessing and database programs; experience with computer applications that involves learning with computers and application skills for desktop publishing and graphics programs; experience with computer applications that involves learning about computers for computer programming and programming languages; experience with computer applications that involves using computers, communication software, and modems to access the Data Information Highway—Telecommunications such as: connection to the Internet, accessing networking links, and use of the World Wide Web.

The experience levels correspond to these application experience categories as follows: Beginning Level—experience with computer applications that involves learning with computers and keyboarding skills for wordprocessing; Intermediate Level—experience with computer applications that ranges across three of the five categories; and Advanced Level—experience with computer applications that ranges across four or more of the five categories.

# Conceptual Framework

## Feminist Standpoint Theory

Feminist theories are varied, reflecting different philosophical and methodological perspectives. However, they all begin with women's experiences and the ways in which those experiences constrain and shape women's lives. Through the lens of feminist research and theory, the classification of female and male not only defines gender, but also influences the nature and type of personal and professional experiences of women and men. Knowledge is rooted overwhelmingly in the lives of men in our society. History is "his story" of events as viewed through the male perspective. There is a need to understand the world through another voice, the women's standpoint. Standpoint theory, which is one of many feminist theories, has strong support in the research of Harding (1991) who has grounded standpoint theory in eight claims. These claims form the basis of the conceptual framework for this study.

Claim One: "Women's different lives have been erroneously devalued and neglected as starting points for research and as the generators of evidence for or against knowledge claims" (Harding, 1991, p. 121). Early feminists sought to fit women's activities and social relations into analytical categories of traditional theoretical discourses, e.g., Marxism, critical theory, psychoanalysis, or functionalism. However, these attempts proved problematic because women's experiences did not provide the grounding for the traditional theoretical frameworks. Women's experiences have seldom generated the problems that traditional theorists attempted to resolve. Research that used women's experiences instead of men's experiences as starting points revealed women's emotional labor, women's "relational" personality structures, and women's different modes of reasoning. The recognition of such phenomena undermined the legitimacy of the central analytical structures of traditional theories (Harding, 1987b).

Millman and Kanter's evaluation (1987) of traditional theories, paradigms, and methodologies indicated the changes that would be needed to reflect both female and male social realities. They found that most of the models that dominate sociology focus upon traditionally masculine concerns and male settings. The sociological emphasis on Weberian rationality in explaining human action and social organization neglected the equally important element of emotion in social life and structure. Traditional theories often assume a single society with respect to men and women in which generalizations can be made of all participants, yet men and women may actually inhabit different psychological and social worlds. Consequently, Harding concludes, women's behavior can not be evaluated by the same (male) criteria as that used for men.

Traditional theorists presumed an essential or universal man who was the subject and object of analysis. Feminist theorists revealed that there is no "generic" man or woman, but vast numbers of men and women living very different lives in historical complexes of class, race, and culture (Harding, 1987). Therefore, traditional theorists who used these restrictive field-defining models, have ignored large chunks of social life. Millman and Kanter (1989) argue that sociologists have focused on "official" actors and actions and have set aside the equally important locations of private, supportive, informal local structures in which women participate most frequently.

> In consequence, not only do we under examine and distort women's activities in social science, but we also fail to understand how social systems function because we do not take into account one of their most basic processes: the interplay between informal, interpersonal networks and the formal, official social structures. It can be argued that sociologists have studied only the tip of the iceberg. (p. 32)

Placing women who use computer based technologies at the center of inquiry in theory and research is essential to broadening understanding about the integration of technology in professional work. Women in education who use computer based technologies have been neglected as starting points for research. Inquiry is needed to understand women's emotional labor, "relational" personality structures, and different modes of reasoning. These three variables are defined briefly as follows:

Harding (1991) defines *emotional labor* as the particular form of any emotion that has a distinct content that women experience as an oppressed, exploited and dominated gender that is missing from all those parallel forms in their brothers' emotional lives. Markus and Oyserman (1989) suggest that societal beliefs condition girls to focus and attend to others as part of the self-definition process. Girls, they suggest, learn to become "exquisitely skilled in being sensitive to others in hearing them, in sharing their internal states, in empathizing with them, and in learning from them" (p. 110). Women use this expertise in knowing what others are thinking and feeling as a basis for action. In contrast, these researchers found that men are conditioned to a separateness self-schema in which their attention is focussed on their own skills, attributes, and talents. The male autonomous self learns by comparing self with others.

According to Harding (1991) *relational personality structures* are understood in reference to object relations theory which points to the less defensive structure of femininity than of masculinity. Gilligan (1982) explains that because girls are parented by a person of the same gender, they see themselves as less differentiated than boys. Therefore they experience themselves as more continuous and related to the external world. "Since masculinity is defined through separation while feminity is defined through *attachment,* male gender identity is threatened by intimacy while female gender identity is threatened by separation" (p. 8). Markus and Oyserman (1989) also found that women are better at fitting or assimilating information into their personality structures. Men, in contrast, are likely to accommodate and change their structures as a result of incoming information, experiencing greater difficulty finding similarity in apparently disparate elements. This difference is attributed to the experience of male children in responding to change and discontinuity in their environment as they free themselves from their early bonding with the female parent.

According to Harding (1991) there are three modes of reasoning characteristic of women not men: the maternal thinking that is characteristic of people who have primary responsibility for the care of small children, the forms of moral reasoning typically found in women's thought, and women's ways of knowing.

*Maternal reasoning* is defined as women's intellectual capacity, judgments, and metaphysical attitudes that are connected by love to preserve fragile existing life, to foster growth, and welcome change (Aptheker, 1989, p. 58).

*Women's moral reasoning* is perceived as "distinctive in women's greater orientation toward relationships and interdependence. This kind of reasoning implies a more contextual mode of judgment and a different mode of understanding" (Gilligan, 1982, p. 22).

Women's ways of knowing, as described by Harding (1991), suggests an intuitive understanding about the ways of human nature derived from the particularity of women's labors with children and men. This psychological understanding may derive from women's focused attention on children and the ways in which children grow and develop personality (Aptheker, 1989, p. 58). Women's ways of knowing also exhibit a concern for context (Harding, 1991).

If we are to understand male and female social realities in the computer culture, narratives are needed to reveal how women's experiences in historical complexes of class, race and culture have affected women's attitudes toward the use of computer based technologies. It is important to hear from women which questions should be asked, which data collected, and which categories should be used in relation to computer based technologies. Have the needs of women been considered in the use of computer based technologies? Do women network and share information with other women? Are women communicating their needs, concerns, and points of view to each other and to the world audience with satellites, cable systems, and video disc and cassette distribution networks? Do women in education explore opportunities to implement computer based technologies in their private lives or in educational and community activities? Studies of women's experiences could open our understanding to locations of private, supportive, informal local structures in which women participate most frequently.

Claim Two: "Women are valuable strangers to the social order" (Harding, 1991, p. 124). Harding finds that there is a gap between women's experiences and the dominant conceptual schemes that are the foundation of our social order. From this gap, women can provide insight into the beliefs and behavior that are invisible in traditional perspectives. As "strangers" to formal knowledge, structures, and frameworks they can more readily identify model biases. Nancy

Hartsock (1983) argues that if human activity is structured in fundamentally opposing ways for two different groups (such as men and women) then "one can expect that the vision of each will represent an inversion of the other, and in systems of domination the vision available to the rulers will be both partial and perverse" (p. 285).

Harding suggests that "starting thought from women's lives" increases the objectivity of the results of the research by bringing scientific observation and perception to bear on assumptions and practices that appear natural and unremarkable from the perspective of men's lives in the dominant groups. "Strangers" who have been excluded from the culture's ways of socializing the "natives" will ask questions about nature and social relations from the perspective of devalued and neglected lives (Harding, 1991).

Quantitative research studies of women and computer based technologies have focussed on gender differences and women's lower levels of computer use. This "inverted" perspective reflects the cultural agendas and assumptions of the dominant group. Objective research requires that women tell their stories. These stories will reveal the hidden cultural influences that will be evidence for knowledge claims relating to gender differences in the use of computer based technologies. What are the social causes of true and false belief systems about women and gender differences with respect to computer based technologies? Thinking from the perspective of women's lives can provide insights into reasons for women's exclusion or acceptance into the computer culture. What cultural agenda and assumptions have shaped and constrained women's use of computer based technologies in early schooling, adult and peer influences, and career choices? What impact does this agenda and assumptions have on the direction and choices of women in education who use computer based technologies?

Claim Three: "Women's oppression gives them fewer interests in ignorance" (Harding, 1991, p. 125). The special subject of feminist inquiry is the "discovery of gender and its consequences." Harding, in *Feminism and Science* (1989b), describes the overarching presence of gender:

> One might even claim that contemporary feminism has "discovered" gender in the sense that we can now see it everywhere, infusing daily beliefs and behaviors that were heretofore thought to be gender-neutral. In boardrooms and bedrooms, urban architecture and suburban developments, the powerful presence and vast consequences of gender now appear in plain sight. (p. 27)

Feminist standpoint theory, in its focus on gender differences, acknowledges the history of oppression in the dominant society and asserts that the condition of dominance provides women with the opportunity to open up knowledge. Harding (1983) classifies manifestations of gender oppression as the *sex/gender system* which she defines as an *organic* variable that organizes social life. Similar to racism and classism, the sex/gender system appears to limit and create opportunities within which are constructed the social practices of daily life—individual expression; the characteristics of social institutions—structural expression; and all of our patterns of thought—symbolic expression. "Feminists' research of 'patriarchy,' 'misogyny,' 'sex-roles,' 'discrimination against women,' or 'the first division of labor—by sex' are 'appearances' of the underlying 'reality' of the sex/gender system" (Harding, 1989b, p. 312).

Women who use computer based technologies work and are educated in diverse social settings. They experience the consequences of gender in these settings and in their daily life experiences. Does gender account for women's oppression in the computer culture? How? Does gender influence the experiences that women recall of denial or access to training in computer based technologies? How? Has gender affected job opportunities and working conditions relating to computer based technologies in education? How?

Claim Four: "Women's perspective is from the other side of the 'battle of the sexes' that women and men engage in on a daily basis" (Harding, 1991, p. 126). Knowledge emerges for the oppressed through the struggles they wage against the oppressors. Knowledge of social reality which results in the feminist standpoint derives from *engagement* in the intellectual and political struggles against male domination (Harding, 1987a). The feminist standpoint is not something anyone can have by claiming it; it is an achievement in the battle of the sexes.

Arpad (1992) describes the personal cost of this knowledge, a knowledge gained by taking a critical perspective of social reality, in *alienation*. "In existential terms, this development of a feminist consciousness means that the person becomes subject, not an object, an authentic self rather than 'the other'" (Arpad, 1992, p. 338). This change of consciousness is a radical change that is disruptive and painful and leads to feelings of estrangement (alienation). Arpad describes this concept of "alienation" as: marginality, being the outsider, betrayal, and estrangement.

Women who use computer based technologies in education engage in this "battle of the sexes" when they challenge traditional social conventions by learning to use this technology. Edwards (1990) states that in America today computer work is a cultural practice, "a large-scale social form that has reinforced modes of thinking, systems of interaction, and ideologies of social control" that are dominated by males:

> In the 1970's, American women entered the higher levels of computer work in ever-increasing numbers. By 1984, 35 percent of U.S. computer programmers and 30 percent of American systems analysts were women. Across the board, in every field of computer work, these percentages continue to rise at varying rates. Yet in spite of these facts, computer work remains a largely male world, one in which women are perceived as unprepared, alien, or unwilling participants. Women are said to perceive the linear logic of computing and the high-tech radiance of its machinery as a hostile and dominating force. (p. 103)

What is the personal cost of computer knowledge to women who enter this world? Do they experience alienation in the family, in the workplace and in the school to achieve this knowledge? What evolution of feminine consciousness has occurred during this process? Women who use computer based technologies in education might be thought of as warriors. (The organizational term for innovators who introduce new technology is "champion"). Research is needed to understand why victories in computer based technologies were possible for these women. What makes them able to strive against their fears to obtain the knowledge of computer based technologies? Were there women champions/warriors in the lives of these women, in their readings, or in their imagination that inspired them to seek self-affirmation?

Claim Five: "Women's perspective is from everyday life" (Harding, 1991, p. 128). Feminist standpoint theory asserts that women's work in every society differs systematically from men's. The institutionalized sexual division of labor specifies how women's lives structure an understanding of social relations. Women's work has a double aspect—their contribution to subsistence and their contribution to childrearing. Women's work differs from men's in that they work longer hours, i.e., the double-day. Women's work also differs in the kinds of work they are assigned that men in the dominant groups refuse to do.  Since women's work relieves men of domestic labor and the care of their bodies, men have time to immerse themselves in the world of abstract concepts.  Men view women's work as a natural activity, a kind of instinctual labor that cannot be compared to real work which involves abstract mental activity.

Women's everyday lives are often fragmented between a job, dinner, and the laundry.  Over time women create meaningful patterns out of the dailiness of their lives as a result of their labors and in the context of their subordinated status to men.  By mapping what they learn and connecting one meaning to another women lay out a different way of seeing reality.  This is what is referred to as a women's standpoint (Aptheker, 1989).

Research is needed to understand the daily life experiences of women who use computer based technologies in education.   What impact does their "double day" and shared responsibilities have on the time they have to use computer based technologies?  What meaning do they give to the patterns in their lives as they work with computer based technologies in their work in schools and in their homes?  Have new patterns emerged in the lives of women who use computer based technologies in their daily work?  Do women who use computer based technologies observe any difference in gender role relationships in their work as a result of this use?

Claim Six:  "Women's perspective comes from mediating ideological dualisms: nature versus culture" (Harding, 1991, p. 128).  Feminist thinkers reject the "dualism of the positive-negative polarities between which most of our intellectual training has taken place" (Aptheker, 1989, p. 18) and assert that the philosophical underpinnings of traditional theories rest on the basis of oppositional thinking.  They hold that the very meaning of the words used to delimit concepts are derived from oppositional contrasts: death versus life; dark versus light; evil versus good, etc. Feminists strive to perceive contrasts as *difference* rather than opposition.  This understanding changes one's perception of reality from polarity and separation to cycles and continua.  For example, Aptheker  reflects on the invention of the traditional Freudian model of the inevitable opposition between mothers and daughters at adolescence.  *"As it was popularized it became prescriptive.*  It was also an invention specific to a historical moment and to Western European, middle-class culture" (p. 18).  When the relationship of mothers and daughters is  perceived as a continuum, women impart to other women the possibilities rather than the limits of their lives.

Lorde (1984) describes what the feminist's respect for difference means:

> Advocating the mere tolerance of difference between women is the grossest reformism. It is a total denial of the creative function of difference in our lives. Difference must not be merely tolerated, but seen as a fund of necessary polarities between which our creativity can spark like a dialectic. Only then does the necessity for interdependency become unthreatening. Only within that interdependency of different strengths, acknowledged and equal, can the power to seek new ways of being in the world generate, as well as the courage and substance to act where there are no charters. (p. 111)

Oppositional thinking is evident in findings from quantitative studies of computer aptitude, attitude, and use. The discussion section of these studies reveals a list of speculations that invariably consist of bipolar interpretations that *invent* gender differences of women's lower levels of computer use. As these results were popularized, they became prescriptive. Women were told they were computerphobic and lacked the mathematical and scientific knowledge necessary to use computers. This grew out of a societal expectation that women were less able in math and science—a whole other area of investigation but nevertheless an antecedent to this (and really, one could go to studies of women in math and science and come to many of these same conclusions).

This study will challenge the gender stereotypes about women and computer based technologies resulting from oppositional thinking. It will reflect the diversity of women in education who come from different backgrounds and reflect different priorities. It will create an affirmation of difference by revealing a *continuum* of women in education who use computer based technologies.

Claim Seven: "Women, and especially women researchers, are 'outsiders within'" (Harding, 1991, p. 7). Feminist researchers have used the historical realities of women's lives as starting points for research. Traditional gatekeepers of knowledge, however, assert that only the impersonal, disinterested, socially anonymous representatives of human reason are capable of producing knowledge. Smith (1987) explains, "Opening an inquiry from the standpoint of women means that women researchers must accept their ineluctable embeddedness in the same world as is the object of their inquiry. It means recognizing that the researcher enters into relationships with others that are structured by relations not fully present" (p. 127). This alternative approach begins with people as subjects who are active and competent and knowers of inquiry. Women researchers are actively present as doers as well as knowers; they are "exploring the dynamic of social relations in which our lives are caught up and which are continually at work in transforming the bases and contexts of our existences and our struggles" (p. 142). Thus the woman researcher is within and outside the problem she seeks to understand. "Her opportunities, her curiosities, as well as her limitations derive from just this necessary standpoint. Her own seeing arises in a context structured by the same system of social relations structuring the everyday worlds of those whose experience provides the problematic of her inquiry" (p. 143).

Thus women researchers are placed in the same critical plane as the overt subject matter. "That is, the class, race, and culture, and gender assumptions, beliefs and behaviors must be placed within the frame of the picture that she/he paints" (Harding, 1989b, p. 29).

This researcher must bear gender too. As a woman educator, I now teach graduate courses in the school of education at an urban college. However, my previous experiences as a teacher and supervisor in inner city schools also influence this research. Reflections on my previous educational and professional experiences, beliefs and practices are a vital part of this dissertation. I also am a user of computer based technologies. The tensions and conflicts generated during this study of women who use computer based technologies will be understood and recorded by an "outsider within."

Claim Eight: "This is the right time in history" (Harding, 1991, p. 132). We live in a transitional culture: feminism is both a product and a cause of the changes underway. In transitional cultures, epistemologies and sciences are frequently in tension with each other. We can look back in history and see that scientists have often used justificatory strategies which their own substantive scientific claims have undermined (sometimes inadvertently). For example, the early modern scientist routinely appealed to religious beliefs as a justification for their science claims; one important reason their claims should be accepted, they said, was science "increased piety and learning" as it revealed in detail the goodness of God's designs (Harding, 1987a, Chapter 12).

Traditional Enlightenment theorists denied that women possessed the reason and powers of dispassionate, objective observation needed for scientific thinking. Women could be the objects of (masculine) reason but never the subjects. Only men were perceived as the ideal knowers, but only men of the appropriate class, race, and culture. Marxism reformulated this Enlightenment vision so that the proletariat, guided by Marxist theory and by class struggle became the ideal knowers. This group, using reason and observation, could grasp the true meaning of social relations. Marxist theory suggested that only one social group, the proletariat, had the knowledge and power to lead. This knowledge, however, could only be generated by the proletariats' struggle in the workplace. Marxism's epistemology is grounded in a theory of labor but not all labor is equal. (This differed from the Enlightenment vision in which not all human reasoning faculties were equal.) But women, in Marxist theory, were never considered full-fledged members of the proletariat who could reason. They were invisible as a class or social group for agents of knowledge (Harding, 1987a).

The epistemological claims of feminist standpoint theory are grounded in a "successor theory of labor, in which women or feminists are substituted for the proletariat as the ideal agents of knowledge. Men's characteristic social experience, like the bourgeoisie, hides from them the politically imposed nature of the social relations they see as natural" (Harding, 1987b, p. 293). Seen from this perspective, the dominant patterns in Western thought justify women's subjugation as necessary for the progress of culture. Women, like the proletariat, are able to use political struggle and analysis to provide a less partial and less defensive understanding of human social relations.

In this transitional world, Harding suggests that Marxist understandings are still regarded as the legitimate ones in the social sciences. Harding indicates that if women's authority in matters of knowledge were already recognized, there would no longer be needed a distinctively feminist social science. Feminist standpoint epistemologies are imperfect. They point to, but do not themselves provide, directions toward a world in which piety toward traditional androcentric authorities will not be the most plausible way to justify new learning (Harding, 1987a, Chapter 12).

We live in a transitional culture: Computer based technologies are both a product and a cause of the changes underway. Feminist epistemologies and computer based technological advances are frequently in tension with each other. Harrington (1993) describes how different computer based activities may generate very different conceptions of teaching and learning, of how we know, and of possible educational futures that are antithetical to feminist thinking.   Damarin (1991) focuses on two epistemological biases inherent in computer based activities:

> Computerization forces a procedural representation of the content to be taught, and thus limits the ways in which subject matter can be understood.  The computer cannot teach nonprocedural ways of knowing, that is understanding through historical, metaphoric, aesthetic, or analogical means. (p. 119)

Computer-based instruction relies on monological discourse in which information is presented to students who are unable to evaluate or analyze it.  This leads to inhibiting students' questioning skills and to the portrayal of information derived from the computer as objective and amoral.  Consequently, students may cease questioning ideas that lead to self knowledge and awareness, and to active participation in the problems in society that need reform.  Bower's critique (1988) of the use of educational computing suggests that computer technology is not neutral in the gender division of society.  Bordo's (1986) analyses of objectivity, Gilligan's (1982) discussion of relationships, and the work of feminist scholars of language supports the argument that especially with respect to gender, computers are not neutral.

Nevertheless, Damarin (1991) suggests that computer technology could be useful in the creation of materials for feminist instruction in mathematics and science.  Harrington (1993) also concurs that applications like computer conferencing can benefit feminist instruction by incorporating activities that build on the communal nature of learning.  "Students will learn through conferencing that how we know is a reflection of what we know, who we are, the experiences we have had, and the 'others' who have been and are a part of it.  Through conferencing students can understand the value and importance of narrative ways of knowing" (p. 10).

Future researchers may seek answers to the next set of questions that are an extension of this present study of women who use computer based technologies in education.  Will women's use or avoidance of computer based technologies bridge the gender gap or augment it?  Will women teachers who introduce computer based technologies to children be the forerunners in breaking the barriers of the sex/ gender system?  Will the significance of gender be evident in a future where computer based technologies dominate everyday living?

## Reflections and Critique of Feminist Standpoint Theory

Feminist standpoint theory is valuable because it affirms that women's daily life experiences have important epistemological consequences for the understanding and construction of social relations. Knowledge is supposed to be based on experience, and women's experiences provide a potential grounding for more complete and less distorted knowledge claims than those in the dominant society. Standpoint theory also recognizes that political struggles are necessary to bring about changes in the sex/gender system to legitimate and empower the "subjugated knowledges" of women. Feminist standpoint theory identifies the common aspects of women's social experiences cross-culturally which contributes to our awareness of the sex/ gender system on a worldwide scale (Harding, 1987b).

Feminist standpoint theory has its limitations. This uniquely feminist perspective is a privileged perspective that favors white, Western, educated women of economic means. Indeed, using the criteria established by the feminist standpoint theorists, there are other groups of men and women whose rights to epistemological claims as subjugated peoples are just as valid. Would not the experiences of the colonized African people—and most especially the African woman—provide the starting points for knowledge about beliefs and social relations? Are race and gender loyalties needed in this representation? Epistemologies based on these groups would offset the need for a privileged feminist perspective.

Feminist standpoint theorists presume a common perspective on knowledge and relationships generalizable across the spectrum of women. But is there a shared perspective among all women? Ask the socialist, the radical, the conservative, the lesbian, the existentialist, the Marxist, or the suburban housewife. Whose voice will represent all other women?

Finally, there are more disturbing aspects of feminist standpoint theory. Epistemological claims based solely on women's experiences seem to retain the problematic features of the sciences they seek to replace. Feminist standpoint theory provides justification for the future establishment of alternative hierarchies that favor women. Does this augur, as Gergen (1988) suggests, that alternative hierarchies will engage in exclusionary tactics that will silence the voices of those who do not consent to the feminist concept of knowledge?

Although the limitations of feminist standpoint theory are apparent, I suggest that the strengths outweigh the weaknesses for the purposes of this study. Feminist standpoint theory opens a set of thematic lenses from which to begin studying this topic. It provides an opportunity to investigate women and their experiences using computer based technologies—not men—whose experiences are already well chronicled.

## Feminist Standpoint Theory— Claims, Clusters, and Applications

Claim One:   "Women's different lives have been erroneously devalued and neglected as starting points for research and as the generators of evidence for or against knowledge claims" (Harding, 1991, p. 121). The thematic lens: Valuing women's experiences is central to this claim. These experiences include: women's emotional labor, women's relational personality structures, and women's different modes of reasoning. What effect do women's unique perceptions have on their use of and experience with computer based technologies? Have these phenomena been considered in understanding women's needs, points of view, and concerns relating to the use of and experience with computer based technologies?

Claim Two: "Women are valuable strangers to the social order" (Harding, 1991, p. 124). The thematic lens: Strangers in this claim refers to women's unique ability as a subjugated group to discern the hidden cultural agenda and assumptions operating in the dominant society. This cultural agenda and its assumptions have shaped and constrained women's use of computer based technologies through early schooling, adult and peer influences, and career choices.

Claim Three: "Women's oppression gives them fewer interests in ignorance" (Harding, 1991, p. 125). The thematic lens central to this claim is oppression /knowledge. Women's history of oppression in the dominant society provides them with the opportunity to open up knowledge about gender and its consequences. The manifestations of gender oppression include the social practices of daily life-individual expression;   the characteristics of social institutions-structural expression; and all of our patterns of thought -symbolic expression. The sex/gender system influences the experiences of women in the computer culture in relation to denial or access to training, job opportunities, and working conditions relating to computer based technologies.

Claim Four: "Women's perspective is from the other side of the battle of the sexes that women and men engage in on a daily basis" (Harding, 1991, p. 126). The thematic lens: Battle gains and losses refers to the achievement of women who attain the true knowledge of social reality, and the personal cost of this knowledge in terms of alienation. As women challenge traditional social conventions in learning to use computer based technologies, they may experience an evolution of feminine consciousness. Have women champions/warriors in their lives inspired these endeavors?

Claim Five: "Women's perspective is from everyday life" (Harding, 1991, p. 128). The thematic lens: Women's work asserts that women's work differs from men's work because of the institutionalized sexual division of labor. Women work longer hours and are assigned the kind of work that men do not do. Women's work and gender role relationships need to be examined in the context of the family and the school as it relates to women's use of and experience with computer based technologies.

Claim Six: "Women's perspective comes from mediating ideological dualisms: nature versus culture" (Harding, 1991, p. 128). The thematic lens: Accepting differences in this claim refers to women's ways of relating to differences in values, cultural behaviors, and thought processes. Women reject the dualism of the positive-negative polarities of traditional thought that rests on oppositional thinking. Rejecting gender stereotypes about women who use computer based technologies, this study will reveal a continuum of professional women in education who use computer based technologies.

Claim Seven: "Women, and especially women researchers, are 'outsiders within'" (Harding, 1991, p. 7). The thematic lens: Seeing from the standpoint in this claim refers to the acceptance of women's lives as starting points for research. Women need not be objects in research, but subjects who are competent knowers of inquiry. Feminist researchers acknowledge that their own perceptions and biases arise from the very same system of social relations that they study. I must recognize that my gender, class, and culture influence my perceptions and gender assumptions as I study and interact with professional women in education who use computer based technologies.

Claim Eight: "This is the right time in history" (Harding, 1991, p. 132). The thematic lens: Theory and science in transition in this claim refer to the fault lines that exist between epistemologies and sciences in times of cultural upheaval. Feminist epistemologies and computer based technologies are frequently in tension with each other. Epistemological biases noted by feminists in computer based activity include: procedural representation of the content to be taught by computers and monological discourse of information presented in computer based instruction. Feminists suggest that computer based technologies can incorporate feminist perspectives. What do women who are professional educators think about the effect of computer based technologies on the students in their classrooms of today and tomorrow?

## *Objectives and Research Questions*

The overarching purpose of the researcher is to investigate the use of computer based technologies by professional women in education through the lens of a theoretical framework that is sensitive to the unique experiences of women. The objectives of this study are:

1. To describe the experiences of these professional women in education who regularly use computer based technologies:
   - To what extent do early learning experiences affect women's use of computer based technologies?
   - How do these women describe their work context and its relationship to computer based technologies?
   - What opportunities have been available for these women to acquire knowledge about computer based technologies?
   - How do these women describe their daily living experiences within the context of the family and its relationship to computer based technologies?
   - To what extent have other women inspired these women to acquire knowledge about computer based technologies?
   - What affect do these women, who are professional educators, think that the use of computer based technologies will have on the students in their classrooms of today and tomorrow?

2. To compare the experiences of these professional women in education who regularly use computer based technologies.

   - How do the descriptions of women's experiences in relation to computer based technologies differ?

   - How are the descriptions of these women's experiences in relation to computer based technologies similar?

3. To what extent does the feminist perspective shed light on the personal narratives of these professional women in education relative to their use of and experience with computer based technologies?

# Chapter II

# The Related Literature

The analogy of research files and computer systems has been used to frame this literature review to delineate aspects of the feminist perspective. The following categories are reviewed: quantitative research studies—the arguments for and against gender differences and computer attitude, ability and use; theory building to new understandings; and qualitative research studies—the new vision of women and computer based technologies.

## *The Argument for Gender Differences That Suggested That Girls/Women Have Lower Levels of Computer Use*

The issue of gender equity in computer education and computer competence in our information age society is considered an important topic in quantitative research studies. However, the underlying presumption of gender-based differences that suggests that women have lower levels of computer use is written as a theme with variations through many of these studies. Grounded in early studies in science and mathematics that documented differences in women's abilities, researchers conducted surveys about gender differences and computer attitude, ability and use thus adding to the empirical evidence that seemed to support this scientific knowledge base. (See Eccles & Jacobs, 1986, and Eccles, 1989, for a review of the literature relating to gender differences in math and science.)

Collis's (1985) seminal study of sex differences in attitude toward computers surveyed 2,899 secondary students. This sample consisted of the entire grade 8 and grade 12 enrollment in one British Columbia school district and a random sample of 50% of the grade 8 and grade 12 enrollment in a second British Columbia school district. The survey consisted of 38 attitude statements-24 related to computers and the remainder to attitudes towards mathematics, science, and writing. Findings from this survey documented the psychosocial implications of gender differences:

> We would like to feel that contemporary young women are confident in their vocational potential and free to choose courses and activities unhindered by gender barriers. We would like to feel that the contemporary female can harmonize needs and wants so that her psychological identity rests on self confidence. But the findings from the 3000 adolescents in this study provide a better fit for the stereotypical profile. Even more distressing, females in this study appeared to be their own enemies; to be more likely than males to stereotype computer use and computer users around a limited and unattractive model and to stereotype themselves as inadequate in the face of technology. (p. 211)

Seven years later, Shashaani (1992) investigated gender-based differences in attitudes toward computers of 1730 secondary students in five different school districts in Pittsburgh, Pennsylvania. In contrast to Collis, Shashaani defined the construct *attitude* as interest, confidence, and stereotype about computer use. Shashaani's review of the literature for her study referred to Collis's study (1985), Hess and Miura's study (1985) of gender differences in enrollment in computer camps, and Martin and Heller's study (1992) of American and Soviet children's

attitudes toward computers. However, Shashaani did not mention any of the available research refuting gender-based differences, but instead quoted several studies that suggested a biological basis for gender differences:

> Hines (1982) relates certain abilities to a biological basis, and argues that distinct hormonal levels and brain functioning (brain lateralization) are the major sex differences in behavior and ability.

Halpern (1986) examined sex differences in cognitive ability by reviewing many related empirical studies and came to the conclusion that biological factors are a significant component in determining sex differences in cognitive abilities. (p. 171)

According to Shashaani (1992), "there is insufficient evidence to show biological inferiority of females in analytical ability" (p. 171). Therefore, the other alternative was to explain the persistence of gender differences in attitudes toward computers as a result of gender role socialization. Shashaani found "that girls, as compared with boys, are less interested in working with computers, lack confidence in using computers, and therefore, have low expectations for success in computing" (p. 179).

Shashaani (1994a) examined the effect of family socioeconomic status (SES), parental sex-typed views and behaviors, and the gender gap in computing. Findings from this new study, which used the same subjects and data derived from the 1992 study, revealed that the persistent gender gap was "essentially social and cultural and not related to inner ability" (p. 446). Shashaani concluded that girls from the low-SES families, are less interested in computers than those from high-SES families, and that parental attitudes and encouragement overshadowed the effect of SES on children's computer attitudes (p. 447). Therefore parents who support females' use of computers are more likely to have girls who use computers.

Shashaani (1994b) also found significant gender differences favoring boys in computer experience, computer class participation, amount of computer usuage, and computer ownership (p. 358). Boys and girls also responded differently in respect to computer use: Boys were more interested in using computers for playing games and writing programs, whereas girls preferred a more application oriented approach; they preferred to use computers for word processing as well as games. Results of this study also indicated that boys who attended more computer classes responded with more confidence in their ability to use computers. However, this relationship was not observed for girls. Therefore Shashaani concludes that taking more computer classes and being familiar with computers may not be enough to reduce the fear and anxiety of girls and build up a level of self confidence for working with computers similar to that of boys. Is this a valid conclusion from this study? Since she gives no recommendations to remedy these findings, is one to conclude that being female means being computerphobic?

Another frequently cited study that provided an empirical base for the anecdotal evidence that technology is a male domain was that of Wilder, Mackie, and Cooper (1985). The subjects in this study were more than 1,600 students in grades kindergarten through 12 in a suburban school district in New Jersey. A questionnaire was administered to all students in which they were asked to select from 50 items those that were sex-typed for girls, those that were sex-typed for boys, and those that were neutral. *The items were read aloud to all students.* This researcher wonders if the gender of the reader influenced the selection of the item? This question was not considered in the research findings. In the middle and high schools, these questionnaires were administered in *mathematics* classes. The researchers concluded: "As predicted, boys and girls alike perceived the computer to be more appropriate for boys than girls, although all responses tended toward the midpoint of the scale. As predicted, there was a sex difference in attitude toward the computer" (p. 218).

Wilder, Mackie, and Cooper (1985) also related the genesis of two other findings that are relevant to understanding attitudes towards computers: They found that girls and boys reported attitudes that were positive toward computers. However, there was also *decreased liking for computers by all students* over time beginning in the sixth grade! In the discussion section, the researchers alluded to this finding and suggested that "school experience has something to do with the changes" (p. 221). The researchers raised the question of how children think about computers when they report that computers are more appropriate for boys than girls: "Are children reacting to the machine (the hardware) or to activities connected with machines (games, instructional software, word processing)?" (p. 222) The researchers state that these questionnaires were administered *individually* to kindergarten, first and some second grade students. This would have been a most appropriate opportunity to ask the children these questions.

Wilder, Mackie, and Cooper (1985) state that the differences between the sexes in attitudes toward the computer are statistically significant, but quite small in an absolute sense. Kay (1992a) notes some of the problems with this study in his analysis of methods used to examine gender differences in computer-related behavior:

> In one study, an impressive sample of 1600 students, grades k to 12, was studied. Unfortunately, all of the results were pooled together. Mean scores would probably be over-or under-inflated, depending

on the proportion of students in each age group. Also, one wonders how a scale could be developed that would address the needs of such a heterogeneous sample. *Results from such a diverse sample should be treated with caution.* (p. 279)

# The Argument Against Gender-Based Differences in Computer Attitude, Ability, and Use

Are there quantitative research studies that indicate that there may be other explanations and results in research on differences in computer aptitude, ability and use? In 1979, the first large scale assessment of computer achievement was conducted by the Minnesota Educational Computer Consortium Assessment Program. According to Anderson (1987), a representative sample of 2,535 Minnesota students in the eleventh grade and 3,615 students in the eighth grade were tested. Early analysis of the results found that males and females performed *equally* well in the domain of general computer literacy. Anderson also analyzed test results for the Programming/Algorithms section of the Minnesota Computer Literacy Assessment and found that *females scored significantly higher than males* in the Problem Analysis subtest. Anderson suggested two explanations for this difference: Students had learned computer skills because the State of Minnesota pioneered projects to infuse computer activities into classrooms, and "women in general may acquire special skills with words and structured thinking that provide an advantage for doing information systems analysis" (p. 48).

Subsequent research providing evidence for female computer competence related to adult women: Vernon-Gerstenfeld's study (1989) examined the effect of learning styles on the adoption of computers in the U.S. Patent and Trademarks Office. The subjects consisted of 95 examiners, a randomly chosen sample from the original population of 1300 patent examiners. Men constituted 85% of the total population and women 13%. A serendipitous finding from this study was that *women showed a greater propensity to adopt computers than men did.* The adoption of computers also *related to a preference for abstract thinking, scientific education, and effective use of training.* Was this an isolated case? Rock, Ekstrom, Goertz, Pollack, and Hilton's studies

(1985) cited in Vernon-Gerstenfeld, found, "females will adopt computers sooner than males when applications, rather than programming, are stressed" (p. 162).

Sacks, Bellisimo, and Mergendoller (1994) examined the relationship between alternative high school students' attitudes toward computers and computer use over a four month period. Computers were used primarily for word processing and computer use was tracked using an internal tracking system. (This was a more precise method of measuring the time students were actually using computers. This was done by using software with a usage tracking feature.) Results revealed that girls' attitudes toward computers improved over the course of the study while boys' attitudes did not. There were no overall gender differences in actual computer use. This study replicated earlier findings that computer experience leads to more positive attitudes toward computers (Arenz & Lee 1990; Chen 1986; Loyd & Loyd 1988.) However, in the current study, such improvement was found only in girls. This study suggests that equal access to computers is essential in generating studies that accurately assess the relationship among gender, computer attitudes, and computer use (p. 267).

Why are there contradictory research findings relating to gender differences in quantitative research studies? Kay's (1992a) critical analysis of 70 studies of gender differences in computer related behavior suggested reasons related to methodology. There were nine areas in these 70 quantitative research studies where common mistakes were made: 1) sample selection, 2) sample size, 3) scale development, 4) scale quality, 5) the use of univariate and multivariate analysis, 6) regression analysis, 7) construct definition, 8) construct testing, and 9) the presentation of results. Kay stated:

> The morass of conflicting results and conclusions permits confusion to reign. Researchers have focused on differences regarding *attitude toward computers* (confidence, interest, motivation, perceived usefulness, locus of control), *aptitude* (general ability, programming, applications and software), and *use* (ownership, experience, courses taken, games, style) in a variety of sub-populations (pre-schoolers, primary, middle school, secondary, and university students, teachers and office employees). The results are conflicting and confusing with the exceptions standing out more than the rules. (p. 277)

Quantitative studies derived from the logical positivist paradigm were supposed to emphasize objectivity and detachment through quantitative methods, i.e., statistical analyses. Indeed, the epistemological belief system inherent in this paradigm asserted, "It is both possible and essential for the inquirer to adopt a distant, noninteractive posture. Values and other biasing, and confounding factors are thereby automatically excluded from influencing the outcomes" (p. 20). But as feminist scholars viewed the skewed results of these quantitative studies relating to gender differences and computer attitude, aptitude, and use in this paradigm, they recognized the need for another reality. The previous files used the MS-DOS operating system. Is there a better operating system that was customized for those women who want postitive results rather than technical mazes that may lead to failure?

Feminist scholars realized that they could not emerge from the silence using the old files; they needed an operating system that contained new files relating to theories that might build new understandings of gender-based differences and computer based technologies.

## *Theory Building to New Understandings*

Turkle and Papert's (1990) research suggested a new approach to understanding gender-based differences and computers that is based on epistemological pluralism. In their study of computer programming, they noted two dimensions of programming: the standard canonical style, which is the conventional route into formal systems through the manipulation of abstract symbols and a concrete and personal style that they termed "bricolage" which uses graphics, sound, text and animation. Levi-Strauss (1968) first used this term to contrast the analytic methodology of Western science with "the science of the concrete" in primitive societies. Bricoleurs construct theories by arranging and rearranging, by negotiating and renegotiating with a set of familiar materials rather than moving abstractly and hierarchically from axiom to theorem to corollary:

At the heart of the new possibilities for the appropriation of formal systems is the computational object, on the border between an abstract idea and a concrete physical object. In the simplest case, a computational object, such as an icon moving on a computer screen can be defined by the most formal rules and is thus a mathematical construct, but at the same time it is visible, almost tangible, and allows a sense of direct manipulation that only the encultured mathematician can feel in traditional formal systems. The computer has a theoretical vocation: it can make the abstract concrete; it can bring formalitiy down-to-earth. (p. 131)

Turkle and Papert's research (1990) of seventy cases, including forty grade school children and thirty college students, found that of the forty grade school children in their study, fourteen girls out of twenty preferred concrete approaches, but of twenty boys only four demonstrated this style preference. They also found that of fifteen women college students taking a programming course, nine were concrete style programmers, but of fifteen men only four preferred the concrete style.

Turkle and Papert (1990) focused on three theories: *feminism, ethnography* of science, and *psychology* (object relations theory) that substantiated the findings that women would feel more comfortable with a relational, interactive, and connected approach to objects, while men react to objects with a more distanced stance, planning, commanding and imposing principles on them. As they observed programmers at work, Turkle and Papert recognized the validity and power of concrete thinking in situations that were traditionally assumed to demand the abstract. They assert that new technological developments such as interfaces, programming philosophy and artificial intelligence may make the computer culture ready to accept epistemological pluralism. Concrete knowledge is considered valuable for it "will open the computer culture to accepting the computer as an expressive medium that encourages distinctive and varied styles of use. There is every reason to think that this pluralistic computer culture would be more welcoming to women and men" (p. 157). Turkle and Papert (1990) indicated that changes will be needed to transform cultural assumptions about the computer from a logical machine that involves technical, mathematical ability to the computer as an artistic tool that people use to write, design, and play with ideas and images:

> Feminist scholarship could make a crucial contribution to the (until now) predominantly male computer culture by promoting recognition of the diverse ways that people think about and appropriate formal systems and by encouraging the acceptance of our profound human connection with tools. (p. 157)

# *Qualitative Research Studies-The New Vision of Women and Computer Based Technologies.*

The alternative paradigm, or worldview (Patton, 1975, p. 9) turns the logical positivist world upside down. There is no longer one reality, but multiple understandings of social reality constricted by time and place bound-knowledge. To capture these realities holistically, researchers moved out of the laboratories and into natural contexts where they could discern meaning in human activity. Lincoln (1990) asserted that "questions of process become critical in new paradigm inquiry" (p. 83). Quantitative researchers perceive knowledge as a hierarchy, taxonomy, or pyramid. Qualitative researchers, however, comprehend knowledge as "clumps of understanding." They seek knowledge of how we know and how we organize what we know (p. 84).

Kay (1994b) studied the process of knowledge acquisition in a computer-based environment. Previous studies on computer ability emphasized the Galtonian perspective of intelligence assessment that involved a predominately linear, construct driven model based on identifying statistically determined factors (p. 403). Binet, however, advocated a dynamic adaptive model of intelligence which emphasized a process approach (Kay, 1994a). If researchers utilized both understandings of intelligence a comprehensive computer ability measure might include:

> Questions about an individual's ability to do a range of tasks, range of experience on a number of software packages and programming languages, and level of formal training. However, most measures include only one or two of these components. Conspicuously absent from these measures are data on how the subject interacts with a computer, the context of computer use, and the goals and needs of the individual. (p. 271)

In the first part of Kay's study (1994b), he conducted two interviews to determine some broad background on the subject's experience with computers and learning in general. This proved important for the analyses and interpretation of the process data he collected in the second part of the study. In this part of the study Kay observed the developmental process of learning a new software package. Kay's sample consisted of 6 adult volunteers (3 graduate students and 3 professionals: 2 males and 4 females). The subjects were videotaped for 60 minutes as they attempted to learn a computer spreadsheet program: Lotus 1-2-3. The first 30 minutes of each of these videotaped sessions was transcribed and included verbal expressions and sounds. Kay examined four components of the knowledge-building process: previous knowledge; task interpretation; problem-solving activities; and errors made (Kay, 1994a, p. 279). Findings were that there was no clear relation between previous computer skills and the completion of the spreadsheet program; subjects used a variety of metaphors (banking, graphs, and games) to apply previous knowledge and experience to new computer tasks; subjects' interpretations of the task (performance goal, learning goal, test, real world work assignment, or evaluation) affected their behaviors and the kind of errors they made; and subjects' use of incorrect computer terminology was reflected in their misunderstanding of new tasks.

It is noteworthy that Kay did not mention gender differences in this study. Yet, four out of the six of his subjects were female and the only subject in the advanced category of computer knowledge and skill was female. What was the reason for not mentioning gender differences?

Kay's previous study (1993) of gender differences in computer attitudes, aptitude, and perceived control suggested the answer to this question. In this study, Kay (1993) employed "statistically reliable and theoretically sound measures"; four instruments were used: Computer Attitude Measure, The Computer Ability Scale, Perceived Control Likert Scale, and The Computer Use Scale. Results of this quantitative study indicated *that there were no significant differences between males and females (647 pre-service teachers) in either affective or cognitive attitudes toward computers.* Males' perceived control over the computer was significantly greater than females' perceived control. Males also scored significantly higher on computer awareness, applied ability, and programming ability. Kay indicated that differences in the relative importance of attitude and ability in predicting male and female use of computers at home and in the classroom suggested *that males and females may view computers differently* therefore, qualitative methodology was needed "to examine the verbal reactions and thinking processes while using the computer, and to examine male-female interaction with computers" (p. 92).

Kay's (1994b) study focuses on verbal reactions and thinking processes; it does not address the issue embedded in his 1993 study: If there is no difference between males' and females' affective and cognitive attitudes toward computers, how are the differences in reactions, thinking processes and interactions with computers to be explained? Answers to these questions may be found in research on the feminist perspective.

Kramer and Lehman (1990) found "documented connections between cultural assumptions, the contexts in which computers are used, and girl's disinterest in computers" (p. 164). For example Scheingold, Hawkins, and Char's study (1984) found that cultural assumptions operate to deny elementary school girls credibility, or even visibility, as competent users, even when these girls demonstrate computer knowledge and skills.

Similarly, Kiesler, Sproull, and Eccles (1985) found that masculine cultural values and stereotypes are incorporated into computer-based learning, work, and play. Their study of high school girls found that girls were passive observers in many computer settings because of the pervasive warlike or competitive sports metaphors in educational and recreational software.

Brownell (1993) investigated the representation of women in computer clip art for the Macintosh computer. He found that of the 1,474 art images, from five different software publishers, identified as human figures 1,388 were categorized as man, woman, boy, or girl. However, a large disparity existed in the clip art representations of men (52.2%) to women (25.3%) (p. 119). These findings suggest that clip art images in computer displays may reinforce the cultural stereotypes that computers are a male domain.

Technological changes are rapidly creating new computer operating systems: Windows 95 slated for the newer desktop and laptop models has revolutionized the computer culture making traditional operating systems obsolete. New software programs are on the market to access the Internet and the World Wide Web. If women are to participate in this new computer age, women need to hear the voices of other women speaking. They need to know the realities of women's computer experiences from the women who have lived them. Therefore, I have attempted to uncloak the silences that have made women invisible in our computer culture. Their voices speak of the use of computer based technologies by professional women in education through the lens of a theoretical framework that is sensitive to the unique experiences of women. Quantitative studies have asked women questions that have little relationship to their life experiences with computer based technologies. Sensitivity to the discepancies in meanings that women perceive might be better understood using Qualitative methodology. In the next chapter I will describe the strategies used to undertake this qualitative research study.

# Chapter III

# The Method

## Qualitative Research

Qualitative research is essentially an investigative process which is as Miles and Huberman (1984) describe it, "is more purposive than random partly because the initial definition of the universe is more limited and partly because social processes have a logic and coherence that random sampling of events or treatments usually reduces to uninterpretable sawdust" (p. 37). Qualitative research is concerned with "meaning." Bogdan and Biklen (1992) define *meaning* in terms of participant perspectives: "They focus on such questions as: What assumptions do people make about their lives? What do they take for granted? By learning the perspectives of the participants, qualitative research illuminates the inner dynamics of situations—dynamics that are invisible to outsiders" (p. 38). Qualitative research is concerned with "thick description" that involves the interaction between culture and the meanings people attribute to events. *Culture,* as defined in this study, is "the acquired knowledge people use to interpret experience and generate behavior. Culture embraces what people do, what people know, and what it is that they know that enables them to behave appropriately in the cultural setting" (p. 38).

This research study is grounded in the Feminist Standpoint knowledge claims of Harding (1991). These eight claims affirm that women's daily life experiences have important epistemological consequences for the understanding and construction of social relations. Harding suggests that if knowledge is supposed to be based on experience, then women's experiences provide a potential grounding for more complete and less distorted knowledge claims than men in the dominant society. The assumption underlying this theory is that knowledge is discovered and justified from field-based inductive methodology. This knowledge is communicated by inside understanding of the perspectives and shared meanings of those in the natural setting or context.

The knowledge claims are abstract propositions embedded in the conceptual framework of feminist standpoint theory. It is necessary to operationalize these claims to develop the research questions. These claims need to be made explicit so that the clusters that emerged could be organized into segments that could be contrasted, compared and analyzed. I searched for the meaning of the claims in the original source materials that Harding referred to in her text, and to other books and articles that she wrote. This process provided the conceptual framework for this study.

After the clusters were formulated from the claims, applications were developed that focussed on the study of women and computer based technologies. Each of the clusters derived from the claims was named: (These thematic lenses were operationalized using the seven photographs as stimuli for the planned probes of the second interview session. Respondents'answers to these probes provided information about the clusters derived from the claims of Feminist Standpoint theory.) Finally, objectives and research questions were developed from the clusters. Thus the beginning of this study employed the deductive model derived from the conceptual framework. But the methodology used in this study is inductive; it is grounded knowledge embedded within the experiences of professional woman in education who use computer based technologies because "it stresses the importance of context, setting, and the subject's frame of reference" (Marshall & Rossman, 1989, p. 50).

# The Setting

The setting is an urban college in the eastern part of the United States. For purposes of anonymity this college will be referred to as Grant College. The real names, locations, and company names will also be changed in the text and in the quotes derived from the transciptions. As an adjunct instructor at this college, I have conferred with the Dean of the School of Education and the Coordinator of the Elementary Education Division about my proposed research on women and computer based technologies. I explained that I would like to interview graduate students and faculty from the college who used computer based technologies. The administrators gave their full cooperation and support.

## Participants

There was a purposive selection of women informants at Grant College to find the best information sources for this study. The following selection criteria were used:

Women were selected because of their experiences with computer based technologies. These experiences were categorized using three levels: beginning, intermediate and advanced. These are not hierarchical classifications but refer to the range of experience across five types of computer applications. These are broad classifications derived from the 20 specific computer experiences charted in the Bank Street National Survey on Telecommunications (Honey & Henriquez, 1993). These types of computer experiences include: Experience with computer applications that involves learning with computers for drill and practice, educational games, etc.; experience with computer applications that involves learning with computers and keyboarding skills for wordprocessing and database programs; experience with computer applications that involves learning with computers and application skills for desktop publishing and graphics programs; experience with computer applications that involves learning about computers for computer programming and programming languages; and experience with computer applications that involves using computers, communication software, and modems for connection to the Internet, accessing networking links, E-mail and the World Wide Web.

The experience levels correspond to these application experience categories as follows: Beginning Level—experience with computer applications that involves learning with computers and keyboarding skills for wordprocessing; Intermediate Level—experience with computer applications that ranges across three of the five categories; and Advanced Level—experience with computer applications that ranges across four or more of the five categories.

Eight participants who volunteered to participate in the study were originally selected because of their varied experiences as professional women in education. Two other subjects agreed to meet with me by telephone, but failed to kept their appointments. Three women volunteered to participate in the study who were in my graduate classes. I explained that only women who were not presently in my classes were acceptable for this study because of ethical considerations. Although I decided that eight subjects would suffice because of limitations on time and means, I added one more participant—a recent immigrant. These women's life stories and their use of computer based technologies form the continuum of women who represent differences in socioeconomic status, ethnicity, and age that I had visualized might emerge from this study.

Participants included: a substitute teacher, a newly appointed teacher, teachers with three or more years of experience, women who were beginning a second career as teachers, a principal, and professors of teachers. The following table describes these participants.

## Table
### Description of Participants

| Code Name | Age | Ethnicity | Experience | Married | Children |
|---|---|---|---|---|---|
| Professor O'Grady | 65 | Irish American | 30 years of college teaching | yes | 7 |
| Miss Lee | 24 | Asian American | 1 year teaching elem. school | no | no |
| Mrs. Intel | 48 | European American | 25 years Computer Programmer | yes | 2 |
| Miss Escuto | 27 | Hispanic American Dom. Repub. | Day care teacher Sp. Ed. | no | no |
| Miss Bell | 45 | African American | 20 yrs. Principal | divorced | no |
| Dr. Goldman | 53 | European American | Director | yes | 2 |
| Miss Garcia | 24 | Hispanic American Puerto Rico | Student Teacher | no | no |
| Mrs. Standish | 31 | European American | 5 yrs. teaching Elem school | yes | 2 |
| Mrs. Varsaw | 35 | Recent Eur. Immigrant | Substitute Parochial school | yes | 1 |

# Ethical Principles in the Conduct of Research

My intent in the conduct of research was to treat human participants with respect and concern. Prior to participation, I informed participants of the nature of the study, i.e., to develop personal narratives about professional women's experiences and computer based technologies. Volunteers agreed prior to the research study that they would participate in three or more taped interview sessions. They were informed that the third session would be a dialogue in which they may respond to the researcher's initial interpretations and findings. Volunteers were selected from students and staff at Grant College. Since I am an adjunct instructor at the college, I ensured the integrity of the study by selecting participants who were not in the classes I was teaching that term. Participants were able to agree or disagree with the research findings without feeling uncomfortable because the researcher was not in a position of authority or influence over them. I also informed participants that they had the right to decline to participate or withdraw from the research at any time.

The participant's right to privacy was an important consideration. Confidentiality was maintained for all respondents. Information received during the interviews was coded so that there would be no link to the respondent's identity. Keys to the code were maintained separately.

Lincoln and Guba suggest that to gain fully informed consent a researcher should prepare a form in advance of the initial meeting with respondents (1985, Chapter 10). This form appears in Appendix A.

# Data Generation

Data collection for this study was accomplished using the In-Depth Interview and Interview Guide. Marshall & Rossman (1989) describe the in-depth interview as a data generation technique that is relied on quite extensively by qualitative researchers. It is "a conversation with a purpose." It is an interaction involving the interviewer and the interviewee in which the researcher explores a few general topics to help uncover the participant's meaning perspective, but otherwise, respects how the participant frames and structures the responses. "The most important aspect of the interviewer's approach concerns conveying the idea that the participant's information is acceptable and valuable" (p. 82).

*Interview Guide* (Preceding the interview, the participant will complete a set of biographical, demographic, and computer use questions. Questions will come from the categories defined in sample choices: Type of user of computer based technologies; education, etc.).

## Session One

After the interviewee was welcomed and seated comfortably, I opened the interview:

The purpose of this interview is to get information that will help me in my research on the lives of women in education who use computer based technologies. As a woman, you are in a unique position to describe your experiences with computer based technologies and how these experiences have affected you. That is what this interview is about: your experiences with computer based technologies and your thoughts about these experiences. Do you have any questions? Please tell me about your experiences with computer based technologies.

My first objective was to allow the respondent to tell her own story in her own terms. "These opening, non directive questions have been named 'grand-tour' questions" (Spradley, 1979, p. 86). This "grand tour question" was the basis of the first session. Detail-oriented, clarification, and elaboration probes were used to deepen the interviewee's responses to questions (McCracken, 1988, p. 35).

Detail-oriented probes were offered in a conversational tone and used to follow up initial responses. They were the basic "who," "what," "when," "where," "how" and "why" questions. These questions were used to complete a detailed picture of an activity or experience. I also used elaboration probes to keep the respondent talking about the subject. It was a simple nod of the interviewer's head to express interest or a more direct verbal response: "I think I'm beginning to understand. Could you say some more about that." Clarification probes were also used to tell the interviewee that I had not fully understood an answer and that more information was needed: "What you're saying now is very important. I think it would help me if you could say some more about that" (Patton, 1990, Chapter Seven).

## *Session Two*

During session two I used the stimulus of "auto-driving." This series of planned prompts was used when the categories that had been identified in the literature review did not emerge spontaneously in the course of the first interview session. McCracken (1988) defines this technique as follows: "The respondent is asked to comment on a picture, video, or some other stimulus, and to provide his or her own account of what they see there" (p. 36). It is usually the researcher who prepares the stimulus material. This is not a projective technique; "it is a prompting strategy that helps to foreground and objectify aspects of the respondent's experiences that are otherwise difficult to bring to the interview" (p. 37).

Photographs of people and computers were selected for use in this study as auto-driving prompts. The following criteria were used in their selection:

1. The photographs depict scenes that reflect life experiences of women and computer based technologies. [The use of photographs that depict women's life experiences have been used in the research of Bunster (1977) to reveal the inner world of feelings, values and significance in the study of Peruvian working women Wex (1979) also used thousands of photographs in her study of women and men in public to demonstrate the differences in women's and men's postures and gestures.]

2. The photographs are used as an auto-driving technique to stimulate responses to the cluster categories derived from the conceptual framework.

3. The photographs were colorful, clear, visual illustrations that tell a story.

I selected these photographs because I thought they would stimulate a discussion of the seven cluster categories and claims of the conceptual framework. I used probes to supplement each of the photographs to elicit information about women and their experiences with computer based technologies. These probes can be found in Appendix B. The photographs can be found in Appendix D.

## *Thematic Photographs*

Bogdan and Biklen (1992) describe the uses of photography in qualitative research. "Photographs provide strikingly descriptive data, and are often used to understand the subjective, and are frequently analyzed inductively. Almost from its advent, photography was employed in conjuction with social science research." (p. 137). These researchers suggest that photographs that are used in qualitive research may be separated into two categories: those that others have taken (Found Photographs) and those that the researcher has a hand in producing (Researcher-Produced Photographs). According to Bogdan and Biklen, Found Photographs may be used "to probe how people define their world: They can reveal what people take for granted, what they assume is unquestionable" (p. 140). These researchers suggest that in the current debate concerning photography's role in social science research Found Photographs that are used as data or stimulant for producing data are the least controversial uses. "The subject of greater contention is the analytic use of photographs; that is, when the researcher claims that the image stands by itself as an abstract statement or as an objective rendering of a setting or issue" (p. 144).

The thematic photographs in this study are photographs from computer magazines. They depict the use of computers by men and women in office and home settings. The photographer or cartoonist is making a statement about the importance of computers in these settings. Feminist standpoint theory is also conerned with these settings of women's daily life experiences. I perceived that they were appropriate to stimulate the responses of the women particpants who were asked to relate their experiences with computers in similar settings.

The first thematic photograph consisted of two cartoons. The first is entitled Working With Windows and the Mainframe Mouse. The man comments to the woman: "This may feel intuitive to you, but it's beginning to make me feel like a horse's patootie." The second cartoon shows a woman saying to a man bent over the computer keyboard: "O.K, Now—This should ease the transition from typing to using a mouse." I thought that these cartoons might be a good stimulus for discussion and an appropriate method to explore women's ways of knowing.). Thematic photograph one can be found in Appendix D.

Thematic photograph two portrays a scene in an elementary school classroom in the 40's or 50's. The little boy in front of the room is holding up his pet frog for his classmates to see. The two girls in the front row squirm in their seats; they sit sideways so that their emotional reactions are visible to an audience. The participants were asked to respond to the photograph and recall their elementary school science experiences. This photograph is the only one that did not come from a computer magazine. It was found in an educational publication. I selected this photograph because I thought it was most appropriate to stimulate a discussion of the respondent's personal experiences in their elementary science classes. This topic was one of the cluster categories relating to the lens on Strangers. Thematic photograph two can be found in Appendix D.

The third thematic photograph reveals an office environment. The large window, floor to ceiling, and huge room might be a loft used for business purposes. Three people are at a desk near the window; a computer is on the desk. Two men are in business attire, but their jackets have been removed. They are both standing in postures of thought. The woman is dressed in a long sleeved shirt and pants or a long skirt. She is wearing boots with a narrow heel. She is seated and seems deep in thought. This photograph came from an advertisement in a computer magazine for office software. I chose this photograph because it portrays a woman engaged in a working relationship with men. The scene suggests that they are using the computer to solve a problem. Another possible interpretation is that they are having a problem using the computer. Whatever the possibilities are, it is apparent that the hands in the photograph indicate that there is a dilemma. I thought this would be an excellent stimulus to determine whether participants view this as a cooperative team situation or as evidence of the sexual discrimination that exists in the workplace, i.e. the woman viewed as the cause of the problem. Thematic photograph three can be found in Appendix D.

Thematic photograph four revealed a darkened room; light was reflected from the screen of two computers and a light source in the hallway. The woman in the foreground was seated at a desk typing in a word processing program. She was wearing a red long-sleeved blouse; her blond hair was long and gathered at the back of her neck in a clip. Her right side profile was visible as she studied the screen. The second woman seated next to a computer was at the far left corner of the room. She was also studying a computer screen. There were two men in the photograph: an African-American who was standing behind the women in the yellow blouse, leaning against a chair, bent forward in conversation. Another male figure was at the open doorway. He appeared as a silhouette. He seemed to be checking a list. The woman respondents were asked which woman in the photograph they would like to be. This photograph was selected because it showed two women working with computers on the job. The older woman was alone in an inner office. The younger woman was in an outer office with a man present. This photograph was selected because it may trigger many different reactions to the thematic lens:   Battle gains and losses. Thematic photograph five can be found in Appendix D.

The focal point in thematic photograph five is an infant dressed in a pink jumpsuit held in mid-air by a woman. The side view of this woman is visible from her head to her shoulders.   She is wearing a black and white polka dot dress or blouse.   The women's attention is concentrated on the infant's expression and/or verbalizations.   At the far left hand corner of the room is a man relaxing in a recliner with his feet up.   He is holding a mouse in his left hand.   The side view of this man indicates that his attention seems to be diverted to the far end of the room.   He is not looking at the woman or child.   A computer sits on the desk next to him but he does not seem to be looking at it although there is a program on the screen.   This photograph was most appropriate to the theme of women's work.   The setting was a home with a father and mother present.   The question:   Do you think this is a working mother?   would be a stimulus triggering responses to the topic of women's work in and out of the home setting.   Thematic photograph five can be found in Appendix D.

Thematic photograph six reveals three central figures; they are a young woman, a young man and an older woman.   Their attention is focused on the Macintosh computer screen that displays the Cole-Haan Case Study with accompanying graphs.   The young girl shares the space in front of the computer with the young man, but her right hand controls the mouse.   The older woman, who might be the teacher, is standing behind the computer; her eyes are directed toward the young girl and her mouth is opened as if she is asking a question or making a statement.   The young boy sits and watches.   In the background are several desktop computers, which seem to indicate that this might be a computer lab.   One male student is visible in the space between the boy and the computer monitor.   Respondents were asked to address three questions:   1)What is the relationship of the women and the girl in this photograph?   2) Why is the woman concentrating on the girl? and 3) Can you describe three women in your life who use computers? This photograph portrays a relationship between the girl and the woman. This was most appropriate to the thematic lens: Accepting Differences.

This would stimulate responses to the question of relationships with other women who use computer based technologies. Thematic photograph six can be found in Appendix D.

There was no thematic photograph for *claim* seven which was "Women, and especially women researchers are 'outsiders within'" (Harding, 1991, p. 7). The thematic analysis of this study in Chapter V would describe my perceptions as a woman researcher.

Thematic photograph seven, was used to stimulate discussion of the cluster category: Theory and science in transition. Respondents were asked if they agree or disagree with the question at the top of the photograph: Improving with Age? There is a typewriter on the left side of the photograph and a computer on the right side. The respondents were also asked to describe some positive effects of computer based technologies in society and in their role as an educator. Next, the respondents were asked to describe some negative effects of computer based technologies in society and in their role as an educator. Finally the respondents were asked to look at the little child on the beach at the bottom of the photograph and predict what changes will be possible in the next twenty-five years with respect to computer based technologies and education, career and life style. This photograph of the beach suggested the wide expanse of unlimited future possibilities. Interestingly, the child on the beach was viewed by some respondents as a boy and by others as a girl. The respondents were asked to view the child as a little girl for this study. This photograph would be appropriate to the thematic lens: Theory and science in transition and would provide the respondents with an opportunity to share their reactions to computer based technologies in our everchanging technological world . Thematic photograph seven can be found in Appendix D.

## Session Three

The focus of the third interview session was a dialogue with each respondent in which I discussed additions, deletions and corrections to the narrative I had written about their experience. The information for this narrative was gathered during the first and second interviews. These follow-up interviews helped to obtain corrective feedback on previously obtained information. It served as a member check on the data and an opportunity for the respondents to exert control over the researcher's interpretations.

Afterwards, I explained the conceptual framework underlying this study. I also gave a summary description of the positive and negative aspects of feminist standpoint theory to familiarize the respondents with the topic and suggest that criticisms of the feminist perspective were acceptable:

> Now, as you know, this research study is about women and computer based technologies. I have two objectives for this research: One is to capture the stories and narratives of women and computer based technologies, and the second is to see if a conceptual framework—the theory that I have selected can shed any light on these personal narratives.
>
> I have selected one of many feminist theories called feminist standpoint theory. Let me give you a short summary of what that's about. Feminist standpoint theory says that women's daily life experiences are important because these different experiences help us to understand social relationships and how they are constructed. Feminist standpoint theory also says that women's knowledge, which is based on their life experiences, has been neglected in research studies, whereas the experiences of men have been recorded and the questions that men are concerned about have already been asked. Third, feminist standpoint theory legitimates and empowers women's thoughts, feelings, and daily life experiences. Last but not least, feminist standpoint theory also recognizes that political struggle is necessary to bring about changes in gender stereotyping.
>
> Now, there are limitations to this theory, of course, and these are two important criticisms: Number one, feminist standpoint theory presumes a common perspective on knowledge and relationships that are generalizable among all women, but that is the debatable issue—do all women share the same perspectives? I don't think so. Second, feminist standpoint theory says that women's experiences are the only true reality, which can lead to a knowledge of exclusion where only those who favor the feminist perspective are accepted. Now, do you have any reactions to feminism or any experiences that you would like to share?

Respondents were then asked to tell me their thoughts about feminism. Mrs. Standish and Mrs. Intel expressed familiarity with the feminist standpoint. The other subjects were not familiar with the theoretical model, but were familiar with the political and economic impact of the feminist liberation movement. (Respondents' comments on the feminist perspective can be found in Chapter IV.)

# Data Analysis

Pfaffenberger (1988) suggests that qualitative data analysis involves three activities: rewriting, coding, and comparison. At the conclusion of each interview session, I devoted time to fleshing out ideas, impressions, and connections. Notes were expanded in a log using Microsoft Word as the computerized field note storage and retrieval system. Reflections after the interview session sometimes produced *breakdown*. This is defined as a lack of fit between one's encounter with a tradition and the schema-guided expectations by which one organizes experience. I resolved breakdowns by creating a new schema that integrated or resolved puzzling statements or seemingly inexplicable behavior (p. 26). This method in which theory follows from the data is known as *grounded theory*. Glaser and Strauss (1967) state that a grounded theory is one that will fit the situation being researched. "By 'fit' we mean that the categories must be readily (not forcibly) applicable to and indicated by the data under study" (p. 3). Their second criteria for a grounded theory is that the categories must also work. "By 'work' we mean that they must be meaningfully relevant to and be able to explain the behavior under study. Grounded theory provides the rationale for working with data that posits multiple realities which cannot be anticipated by the researcher working in the field.

The analysis of the data in this study was a process that began with the preservation and collection of data during interview sessions that were taped and later professionally transcribed. Reduction of the data was accomplished through the use of *Folio Views*, a computer software program that helped in the management and categorization of the data. Coding categories were initially developed from the cluster categories and then modified to suit the new understandings of the data that emerged. As I discovered new codes and created typologies to sort the data a framework of theory emerged. This is what Glaser and Strauss (1967) refer to as grounded theory. The computer software program, *Folio Views*, stored the data and provided ease of retrieval through the use of shadow files which left in tact the original transcript. I was able to analyze and highlight coding categories through the use of Query and Highlighter. New categories could be identified and all the strips containing those category codes could be highlighted using a combination of colors and fonts. Using query I was able to easily group the new coded units. Thus this computer program permitted a flexible and evolving set of coding categories. Notes on new insights could be easily attached using the icon in the left margin. Links from one category in the infobase to another were possible using Popup links and Jump links. Miles and Huberman (1994) evaluated twenty two computer software programs. *Folio Views* was given a high rating for user friendliness. It was also rated "Strong" on Coding, Search and Retrieval, Database Management, Memoing, and Data linking (p. 316). I found this computer program to be all of the above. I was especially interested in the Create function which allows the user to develop Infobases from files in other programs. This program was most helpful in the data reduction and interpretation phase of my research.

## *Coding: Descriptive and Interpretive*

The first round of coding and categorizing determined the respondent's view of the world in general and the topic in particular from the first interview session. These codes were descriptive codes. I found thirteen main code categories from this first round and 70 descriptive codes. The second stage of coding examined the interconnection between the observations of the first round, and the clusters derived from the theoretical framework. Additional clusters that emerged from analysis of the first round were added at this time. Clusters that were derived from the eight lenses of feminist standpoint theory were modified during the research process.

## *Comparison*

As researcher I was the "human" instrument in the analysis of qualitative data derived from the interview sessions. In the first stage of analysis the researcher "acts more like an archaeologist, sorting out important material from unimportant material with no attention to how the important material will eventually be assembled" (McCracken, 1988, p. 44). I used the data from interview session one as an entranceway into the assumptions and beliefs of the respondent. I had to reflect and decide on the coding categories derived from the transcripts. I had to select the photographs that I believed reflected the thematic lenses. My reflections upon a stream of associations evoked by the data helped me to develop insights into the meaning of the data (p. 45).

During the second stage of the analysis process, I used the seven cluster categories derived from the conceptual framework as a template against the coded categories derived from the data in the first and second transcribed interviews. I searched for relationships or similarities evident in the data. Then I went back to the the data derived from the three interview sessions to develop a thematic analysis for each case. Patterns and themes sometimes emerged that were appropriate to more than one data strip. Working from the computer coded transcriptions saved space and time, but I also found it necessary to leave the computer screen and work with the original paper transcripts of the data. I read this material through many many times to try to review my thoughts about the meaning of the words used by the respondents in the context of our discussions during the interviews. Afterwards the themes derived from each of the cases were categorized using the original research questions.

The third stage was a time of judgment in which I analyzed all the respondents' themes for each of the seven research categories and searched for new understandings. After a lengthy period of immersion and reflection I was able to draw out new understandings from a comparison of each category and the themes that emerged. This is presented as a cross-case analysis derived from the thematic analysis of each of the nine cases. This cross case analysis is found in Chapter V.

The fourth stage of this analytical process involved returning to the original claims in Feminist Standpoint theory as a basis for analysis and pattern matching of the data. The findings from the cross-case analysis were matched against the claims to shed new light on the narratives of women who use computer based technologies. It was at this time that I also found it necessary to bring together several of the claims that were similar. The results of this analysis are also found in Chapter V.

## *Establishing Trustworthiness*

McCracken (1988) asks: How does the investigator ensure the quality of his or her own qualitative research? If qualitative research cannot be judged by quantitative standards, what criteria are used to determine the trustworthiness of a study? The major criteria established by qualitative researchers are credibility, dependability, and confirmability.

Lincoln and Guba (1985) suggest that the "truth value" of the study can be demonstrated through the credibility criterion which involves a two-fold task: "first, to carry out the inquiry in such a way that the probability that the findings will be found to be credible is enhanced and, second, to demonstrate the credibility of the findings by having them approved by the constructors of the multiple realities being studied" (p. 296).

Therefore the findings should reflect the multiple realities of the respondents, rather than an imposed reality suggested by the researcher. The findings should present an authentic picture, uncontrived, and unmodified by the researcher's actions.   I endeavored to enhance the credibility of my study by prolonged contact with respondents to develop context-rich and meaningful (thick) descriptions.   Three interviews were used for this purpose.   I employed the technique of triangulation among multiple data sources during interview three to ensure accuracy of the information presented in the narratives.   Respondents were asked to add, delete, or correct information contained in the narratives which were developed from interviews one and two.   A summary of the additions, deletions, and corrections are given for each respondent as well as the number of transcribed pages resulting from interviews one and two.   I also worked closely with my committee members who gave me invaluable advice involving comments, corrections, and bias checks. Credibility was further enhanced by attention to the details of data collection, data processing, and data analysis.   Every aspect of this study:   coding, categorizing, noting patterns and developing themes were all involved with the issue of credibility (Miles and Huberman, 1994, p. 278).

## *Dependability*

Dependability is understood by qualitative researchers as "the process in which the researcher attempts to account for the changing conditions in the phenomenon being studied, as well as changes in the design created by new understandings of the settings" (Marshall & Rossman, 1989, p. 147).   It differs significantly from the concept of reliability in quantitative research in which replication of a study is possible in an unchanging universe.   I have used the "audit trail" for this purpose.   It   was a detailed record of the study's methods and procedures that I followed.   This information was written using my computer.   It is a detailed account of the interview sessions and reactions to these sessions. It also contains the methods I used to place the transcribed data into *Folio Views*—the computer software program that was used to code the data. I describe a detailed step by step approach for the use of *Folio Views* to create an infobase. This description may help another researcher who wishes to use this software computer program in a qualitative study. A sample of the Audit Trail can be found in Appendix C.

Miles & Huberman (1994) suggest other procedures relevant in this domain: "Basic paradigms and analytic constructs need to be clearly specified so that the reliability of the findings can be connected to theory" (p. 278). In this study, the claims of Feminist Standpoint theory have been operationalized through the cluster categories and applications which relate to women and the use of computer based technologies. Thematic lenses highlight the claims and are used throughout this research.

"The researcher's role and status within the site should be explicitly described. Data should be collected across the full range of appropriate settings, times, respondents, and so on as suggested in the research questions" (p. 278). My role as an adjunct instructor was noted. This role provided the opportunity to ask for volunteers from the graduate students and faculty who wished to participate in this study. Three interviews were given to each of the nine participants. Therefore, twenty seven interview sessions were taped, transcribed and coded. Each case was analyzed separately and then the thematic elements of each case were compared in a cross case analysis so that similarities and contrasts of respondent's answers to the research questions relating to the Feminist Standpoint claims were easily identifiable.

I also wrote a personal journal to further enhance dependability by recording my observations and personal thoughts. This journal also kept me on target as I moved through the different phases of this project.

## *Confirmability*

Confirmability in qualitative research depends upon the neutrality of the researcher in providing controls for bias in interpretation (Marshall & Rossman, 1989, p. 147). Findings from the study must be grounded in the data not in the biases or motivations of the researcher. I have used the audit trail and the transcripts which were done professionally to strenghten the confirmability of this study.

Another technique I incorporated was the third interview session, in which there was a dialogue between this researcher and individual respondents concerning the accuracy of the research findings. This dialogue was used to confirm the reconstruction of the respondent's perspectives. Miles & Huberman (1994) suggest the following procedures in this domain:

> The general methods and procedures of the study should be described explicitly and in great detail, including "backstage information." The researcher must be explicit and as self aware as possible about personal assumptions, values and biases, affective states, and how they may have come into play in the study. (p. 278)

In qualitative research, the researcher serves as an instrument in the collection and analysis of the data. This metaphor suggests that the researcher uses a broad range of personal experiences, imagination, and intellect in ways that are various and unpredictable. For example, I selected the thematic photographs used during interview two to open the lenses of the conceptual framework. There were many pitfalls in this sorting and winnowing of data in this study that underlie the criteria of truthfulness. The feminist methodology that frames this study suggests specific ways for gathering evidence. It is based on the epistemological claims that suggest that women are the knowers or agents of knowledge. Therefore it is women's experiences that provide the new resources for research. These experiences are the reality against which hypotheses are tested. These constructions of reality which inform women's thinking are separate and distinct from men's. I wondered as I began this reseach if women would speak of their personal lives to another woman. Would they value my presence as a researcher? What would their reactions be when they were informed that I was doing research from a feminist perspective? I also wondered whether I would be able to see their reality from a feminist standpoint? These women come from many different classes, races, and cultures. They span generations. Was there a basis for understanding and communicating about gender issues? Would I be able to accept their perceptions of their subjective reality as truth? These were the issues that I wrestled with as the outsider within. I also had to maintain distance during this research process and not over identify with research participants. Furthermore, I was constantly on guard against fitting the respondents' observations, procrustean-like into the theoretical framework. Negative instances were searched for and acknowledged.

## Chapter IV

# Women of the Computer Generations

Computer history is marked by four technological generations. First-generation computers used vacuum tubes as the primary electrical component. The second-generation computers were made of transistors, and some commercial models featured compilers. Third-generation computers were composed of integrated circuits and featured standardized architecture, which permitted upward compatibility of software. Fourth-generation computers rely on large-scale and very large-scale intergrated circuits, and they process by using realtime systems.

*Computing Concepts*, Duffy & Berchelmann, 1995 (p. 23)

These are the stories of women whose lives spanned four computer generations. Women, whose beginnings are from different historic complexes of class, race, and culture, yet they all share this extraordinary opportunity in time: to learn about and use computer based technologies. These nine professional women in education have agreed to share their stories through a series of three interviews that have been recorded and transcribed to develop personal narratives of professional women in education and their use of and experience with computer based technologies. The data derived from these interviews have been organized into three sections: participants' narratives based on interviews' one and two; participants' responses to the probes (see Appendix B) and photographs (see Appendix D) during interview two;

and participants' check of the narratives and reactions to the feminist perspective during interview three.

## *Professor O'Grady*

Professor O'Grady is a senior professor in the Department of Education. She is an Irish American, age 65, married, and the mother of seven: five daughters and two sons. Her college responsibilities include teaching courses and administering the reading program, which includes about one hundred students in six different sections. She is also a consultant and evaluator to school districts in reading. Professor O'Grady is one of the few full time faculty members in the Department of Education who uses computers.

She began her computer experience as a Ph.D. candidate in 1967. She was one of the first students at her doctoral institution to use a computer program. Her data were placed on punch cards which were used in first generation computers. (The perforations on each of the columns on the card indicated a specific digit, alphabetic character or other symbol. Some programs required thousands of cards to be fed in batches into the computer, to be read by a processing device that had mechanical fingers to sense the holes in the card.)

> In 1967, I was the first candidate for a Ph.D. who was allowed to use a program. I didn't understand the program too well but I was allowed to use it and all I had to do was do my keypunch and then make sure the cards were lined up. I put them in the machine and took them out. And then at my defense, I had to defend the fact that I understood statistics well enough that I could use the computer instead of a Frieden calculator.

But this was not her first experience with computers. When she was graduated from high school, her father was sick and she had to work to help support the family. She found a job in an insurance company where they had a computer that took up a whole room: "They had to wire the board physically . We would tell them what we wanted and then a little man would come with a big board and would go: 'positive,' 'negative,' 'in,' 'out'—binary language. That was way back in '47 to '52."

She worked at a large insurance company during the day and attended classes at the college in the evening. It took her five years to complete her Bachelor's degree in Latin and German, which also included thirty-six credits in philosophy. Professor O'Grady thinks that if she had stayed at the insurance company she might have been an actuary today; but she had always wanted to be a teacher:

> I had one brother and two sisters. I was the oldest. I used to take them outside when we played house and certain weeds were spinach and certain weeds were asparagus. And then I would take them around the other side of the big rock and that became a school, and I would teach them their lessons.

Professor O'Grady feels that her father encouraged her to study and she recalls:

> In high school I had a cute little nun in the library who said to me, "What's your name?" I told her and she said, "Oh my goodness, that's the name of a famous Irish Queen," and boy she was really something special. "Let me get the book," and she got the book and showed it to me. And all along the way there have been nuns, like the one I told you about, who got her doctorate in 1935.

Professor O'Grady earned her Master's in Ed Psychology in the evening while teaching during the day. Then, she transferred to an elementary school in New Jersey. While there she went on to get her doctorate in Elementary Education with a specialty in Reading. "They said if you want to stay here you need state certification; you have to get thirty-six credits of elementary education. So I said, 'Well, all right, I'll go get a doctorate,' so that's what I did. I had no guidance."

As she was completing her coursework for the doctorate, she met her future husband. In 1967, she was appointed to a professorship at Grant College in the Department of Education. Professor O'Grady recalls the ten years between 1957, when she completed her coursework and 1967, when she finished her dissertation, that she devoted to raising her children:

> You're ten years behind in your career. And when I was coming up for full professor, I was coming up with colleagues whom I value highly, who were at least ten years younger than I was. But I made a conscious decision when I was getting tenure and was an assistant professor that my first priority was the children. I would do the minimum to get tenure and fulfill my responsibilities to the job, but not to the push you needed to get promoted. That came later.

Many years later, Professor O'Grady renewed her interest in computers when one of her daughters gave her an old IBM computer and another taught her WordStar, which is an "antedeluvian word processing program." (In 1979 MicroPro International introduced WordStar, one of the first full-featured word-processing packages for the microcomputer. In 1981 MS-DOS became the standard disk operating system for the IBM PC.)

Professor O'Grady's initial experience with computers was frustrating:

> I would sit there and work, and then when I would get frustrated I would cry, because I would have lots of little letters that I didn't want trailing along with what I wanted, and I didn't know how to get rid of them until I found that you hit "Control G" and then I became a lot happier. And I figured out how to set up a file and to write it and print it out, which made me very very happy.

During the time that Professor O'Grady was honing her typing skills using DOS, she was observing the use of computers in schools as a supervisor of student teachers. She found great disparity in what she observed:

> I was looking at computers in schools, and what I found there, and the research seems to bear me out, was that in middle and upper class schools, computers were used with the children in a way for them to learn how to program and as a word processor, and to do very sophisticated kinds of experiences with computers. Lower class children in ghetto areas, at risk children, where computers were available, they were used for drill and practice. For example, The Write to Read program that I saw in a school in Westchester was very sophisticated. This same program that I see in schools in our city is a lot of drill and practice which is very disappointing. So in my professional life, I had a cause now to get kids away from drill and practice to using computers as a learning tool to generate children's writing.

Professor O'Grady's professional life also offered an opportunity to learn programming from the Chairman of the Computer Information Science Department at the college. Many people dropped out of this course, but Professor O'Grady persisted in doing all the assignments— although she got them wrong "all the time first off." "He used to look at me and say, 'You're really not too bright lady, you know? You're putting men in with women or smokers with non-smokers.' I was doing awful things." But she persisted staying there until 11:00 and 12:00 at night. Humorously, she explained that the three hundred dollars she received and the hours she spent added up to a dollar-fifty an hour. Although she never used the programs she developed that summer, Professor O'Grady thought that the course gave her new insight into the logic behind programming. "The language model used was PL-1."

Professor O'Grady also used the computer lab that was available to faculty. She met "a very nice young man named John" who helped her. When she recently bought her new Compaq computer that opened to the program manager screen of Windows, she called this same young man for help:

> And when I got my new computer, I said, "John, you have to come over and clue me," so he came over, and he's the one who got rid of the big Folios on Windows and set it up so that I can go directly to DOS and the "C" prompt. Then I opened my files, and switched them over to the the "A" drive and back to the "C" drive. And he made me very happy, so John is my pal.

Professor O'Grady's children who gather together at her home to "play on Prodigy" also offer help and advice: "They say, 'Oh Ma, you should use it. Ma, you got a fax, you got a modem; this is a very sophisticated computer.'" But she says that at the present time she is just trying to complete her course outlines. However, she has almost completed the book she is writing using the wordprocessing program on the computer.Professor O'Grady was very much aware of each of her children's uses of computers:

> [*Mary, college professor, age 38*] Mary, she works with tapes from the Federal government on demography (the census) and knows all kinds of languages and is very sophisticated on the computer. [She gave Professor O'Grady her first computer.]

> [*Michael, teacher, college professor, age 36*] Michael is very interesting. He's an Apple man (Macintosh) and he's a musician. He has programs that allow him to write music on his computer. His wife, who is a professor of music, has her own computer. They have graphics and everything.

[*Ann, Ph.D. candidate, age 35*] Ann is number three. She's the one who tutored me. She's a Ph.D. candidate so she's very sophisticated with using computers to store data.

[*Tom, Insurance Salesman, age 34*] Tom has a laptop and he does a lot of spreadsheeting and work like that, but mostly, his wife says, he likes to play solitaire on the airplane with his laptop. Tom plays Crayola and programs like that with his little guy, so this four-year-old is probably going to be very sophisticated with computers.

[*Liz, post Doctorate—Biology, age 34*] Liz uses the computer in her research on heat shock at the molecular level to seed in plants.

[*Margaret, age 33*] Margaret is the writer of computer manuals. And they're all on "E"-mail to one another, so if anything happens—they send the word around.

[*Joanie, lawyer, age 30, Lawyer*] Joanie uses CD-ROMS for research in law and all of that. She's pretty sophisticated.

Professor O'Grady's husband, who is a college professor, was just beginning to learn about computers.

Professor O'Grady recognized that time is needed to learn about computer based technologies; but she would like to apply the knowledge she now possesses. She wanted access to a computer in her office:

> I would keep a good record of the students in my program—their courses, their status, etc. Then there is a computer program that I want to buy: The D.R.P. Readability Program. It costs about five hundred dollars. If I had that computer program set up in my office, I could invite my students to come in and type a passage and get its readability, which would be wonderful for choosing a textbook or practice materials. I have a computer at home, but what good is it at home? I'd have to have my students come in the back door every night. It should be here at the college. I don't feel I get any support from the college. My secretary runs across the hall to type memos on their computer. I don't even have a typewriter. Oh, they do have a computer in the mailroom for faculty use, but we can't use it because they have it double locked because of security. So what can you do? If I had a computer in my office , you know, that's all I can think of that would make my computer life a little bit better.

## *Responses to the Probes and Photographs*

### *Photograph One*

Professor O'Grady stated that she believed that there were no differences between men and women with respect to computer ability. She thought that people have equal stores of knowledge but that each person is an individual.

She considered herself knowledgeable about teaching reading, child development and architecture. Her husband however, was knowledgeable about history, biography, baseball and accounting. She believed that the research of Johnson O'Connor indicated that women's brains function differently from men's brains. According to the research women are more verbal than men and men are more spatial than women. She did not like the word "intuition" but in her analysis of how she solves a problem, she stated that she does jump to conclusions and then backtracks and solves the problem logically—step by step. This was her approach to the initial computer learning experience. She had to realize that she was smarter than the computer and then instead of crying she analyzed the situation and found the code keys that corrected the error.

### *Photograph Two*

Professor O'Grady did not remember if she had science classes in elementary school but she did a lot of "natural stuff" outside of school. She remembered visiting the Bronx Zoo, walking along the river edge, and keeping polliwogs that later turned into frogs.

She had wonderful science teachers in high school. One of her teachers, was a nun who received her Ph.D. in Science in 1935. Professor O'Grady remembered working with her on a project involving mushrooms. She also remembered helping her children with science projects at home.

When she was a child, Professor O'Grady remembered playing house and school with her brothers and sisters. She always wanted to be a teacher. "I used to take them out, and certain weeds were spinach and certain weeds were asparagus, that's when we played house, and then I'd take them around the other side of the big rock, and that became the school, and I would teach them their lessons." She remembered leaving high school and having to go to work because her father was sick and she did not even have the carefare to go to college. She worked in an insurance company and might have been an actuary today, but she wasn't interested in the job because she wasn't "a policy-form person." She wanted to teach. She completed college in the evening and went into teaching. Afterwards she went on to get a Masters in educational psychology. She recalled transferring to a teaching position in New Jersey because the salary was higher. When the administration told her she needed thirty-six credits in elementary education she decided to get the doctorate. She met her husband just as she was completing the course work for the degree. She expressed the desire to return to teaching elementary school where she would teach little girls, like the ones in the photograph, not to be afraid of "frogs and things."

### Photograph Three

Professor O'Grady thought that the role of the women in the photograph was not a "head honcho" but a problem solver. She reflected that while the men were becoming agitated, the woman was working on the solution.

She described how being a woman affected her career. She had taken ten years out to have her family, and when she returned she was ten years behind. She recalled coming up for full professor with colleagues who were ten years younger than she was. She also remembered making a conscious decision as an assistant professor to make her family her first priority.

She indicated that the hardest part about being a woman on her job was dealing with difficult women. These women had taken the feminist position to the ultimate and she had to deal with the students who were having problems with these professors.

### Photograph Four

Professor O'Grady said that she did not see the advantage of being one woman or the other in the photograph who was using the computer. She did believe, however, that word-processing on the computer was a great improvement over typing. She remembered taking a course in programming that taught her to be logical. She stated that she needed time to learn to understand and use America-On-Line and learn how to E-mail notes to her children. Then she described an interview on "Wall Street Week" in which the guest, who represented a mutual fund, said he would never buy stocks in technology companies because things change too quickly. She agreed because her son-in-law and daughter work for technology companies and they are under constant stress because of the rapid changes that are taking place.

She explained that her children motivated her to learn to use the desk-top computer. One daughter gave her an old computer and her son started to learn about computers at the same time she did. Her husband had a new job this year and the college where he worked gave him a computer and a tutorial on how to use it. But he still asks her to type up letters he needs. She has a set of files with his name on it.

Her colleagues in the department were not interested in computer based technologies. However, in math classes they used computers to evaluate software but they did not teach programming. Professor O'Grady indicated that she asked the department for a computer for her office. In fact, her secretary did not even have a typewriter. She wanted to buy a D.R.P. Readability Program that her students could use to determine the grade level of reading passages. She did not feel that she received any support from the department on these requests. Computer networking in her department is a problem. The question "Do you use a computer?" is equivalent to the personal question "Do you still beat you wife?"

### *Photograph Five*

Professor O'Grady did not think the woman in the photograph had to be a working mother. She thought that the woman in the photograph could use the computer for storing recipes, preparing a shopping list, of writing the Great American Novel after the children go to bed.

Professor O'Grady described her work responsibilities. She taught courses and was in charge of program administration for the reading program. She was also a consultant in reading to school districts. At home her responsibilities included all the household chores. She indicated that her husband takes out the garbage and sometimes goes shopping with her. He also takes his clothes to the cleaners and his shirts to the laundry. She cooks for the family on the weekends and shares the responsibility with the Chinese takeout and the Italian-takeout during the week.

### *Photograph Six*

Professor O'Grady suggested that the woman in the photograph might be a professor and the young man and woman her students. She thought they might be involved in a discussion about the case study on the computer screen.

Professor O'Grady described the work of three women in her family who use computer based technologies. Her daughters who were sophisticated computer users. She also mentioned a former student whom she encouraged to get her doctorate in mathematics. This student has since been employed to teach computers at Grant College.

Professor O'Grady described the inspirational women in her life, a nun she met in the library who cared enough to tell her that she had the name of a famous Irish Queen, and her science teacher in high school who had the doctorate in 1935. These women were inspirational in terms of "intellectual life." Her mother, however, used to say, "I don't know what you're spending all that money for, you're wasting your time; you'll get married; you'll never do anything." Professor O'Grady said, "She was not encouraging of professional growth." She also indicated that her father encouraged her to study. She remembered one professor who was very supportive when she first came to Grant College. But she was disappointed in the support she received from women in her profession.

## *Photograph Seven*

Professor O'Grady expressed mixed reactions to the photograph title: "Improving with Age?" She said she had problems filling out forms, but she found great advantages to using computers over typewriters: "The ability to share your knowledge and organize your knowledge has improved with technology." She also appreciated the mobility of a laptop that you can use without electricity. The only negative effect, Professor O'Grady expressed in reference to computers, was the differential use that educators made of computer technology, depending on the social class of children. In middle class neighborhoods however, children were introduced to Basic, a computer language, or Bank Street Write. However, she observed that in ghetto neighborhoods the computers were just used for drill and practice.

Professor O'Grady expressed concern over the problems that women were facing today in terms of responsibilities for children, home, and career. She predicted that one day women will be working from home with material that can be "FedEx'd" to them. She believed that that would be a freeing up for both husband and wife.

Professor O'Grady did not believe that computers would revolutionize education. She thought the essence of education and teaching was the interaction of person to person.

*Interview Three*

My purpose in the third interview was twofold: to provide an opportunity for each respondent to correct, add, and/or delete information in the constructed narratives and to open a dialogue on the feminist perspective by revealing the conceptual framework for this study. This dialogue attempts to assure the confirmability of the findings through "member checks."

Professor O'Grady suggested one correction, two additions, and no deletions to the seven pages of narrative describing her experiences using computer based technologies:

*Correction one* was the correct name of the university she graduated from.

*Addition one* was the change from "I did not understand the program at all" to "I did not understand the program too well."

*Addition two* was the sentence—Between finishing coursework in 1957 and completing the dissertation in 1967 she was home with her children.

She was shown the transcriptions from interviews one and two used to develop the narrative. There were 14 transcribed pages from interview one and 47 transcribed pages from interview two. As she read the narrative she expressed surprise at the varied experiences she had with computers over her life time.

Then I gave a descriptive summary of feminist standpoint theory and asked her for reactions or experiences relating to the feminist perspective. Professor O'Grady stated that she knew "absolutely nothing about feminist theory. However, she had always believed that Kohlberg's work on the development of moral reasoning was not valid with reference to women. Although Kohlberg found that women never get to the highest level of moral reasoning, Professor O'Grady indicated that the choice of questions he asked was not within women's experiences. If the questions were within women's experiences, Professor O'Grady believed that women would have reached the same moral development as men.

She stated that she was uncomfortable with the feminist philosophy because she didn't fit the mold since she had a career and many children. She reacted to the group of feminists that she knew who were in favor of abortion and birth control. She believed that women were entitled to have the number of children they wanted and the number of children they could care for.

Professor O'Grady stated that there was a glass ceiling, and that women were not valued intellectually for themselves. In fact, they were seen as good looking women first, and then, "What else do you know?" She thought that women have not been supportive of other women the way they could be (Transcript: Interview III, p. 15, 5/17/ 95).

## Mrs. Intel

Mrs. Intel is a second career student in education at Grant College. She was a former computer programmer, system analyst, and project leader. She is a European American, age 48, married, and the mother of two sons.

Mrs. Intel's interest in computers was launched in 1964 when her boyfriend introduced her to first generation computers:

> I had a boyfriend in 1964 who was a graduate student at a university, and he was using computers where we used bits and bytes, zeros and ones. He had these long huge stacks of print-outs, and he showed me about machine coding. I found it very intriguing at that time.

In 1979 Mrs. Intel began taking courses at this university in COBOL and main frame assembly language which involved the use of second generation computers:

> [The transistor made possible a new generation of computers that were faster, cooler, and more compact. Second generation computers used magnetic cores instead of magnetic drums for internal storage. COBOL (COmmon Business-Oriented Language) became commercially available. Business began to apply the computer to basic record-keeping tasks like inventory management, payroll, and accounting. Grace Hopper developed the first COBOL compiler, which allowed COBOL programs to be run on many separate computers.]
> *Computing Concepts*, Duffy and Berchelmann, 1995 (p. 13)

Mrs. Intel's first job after completing her courses was at a large stock-clearing house. "It was a good high tech environment, reliability was considered important, so I learned good techniques." Her responsibility involved keeping track of stock transfers as trades were settled for banks and brokerage houses. She started as a trainee, moved up to programmer, and then on to systems analyst. "In 1980 when I started as a trainee, all the women trainees, regardless of education, started at an average salary of fourteen thousand dollars a year, and the males started at twenty thousand dollars regardless of educational level. This was the phenomenon of the time." She stayed on this job until something happened that made her decide to leave the company:

> At some point, I stopped being included in the new projects, and I sensed a kind of closing in. Finally my boss told me that he didn't believe in promoting women any further because they didn't make good managers because they worked too hard and drove their staff. So I started looking for another job.

Her job search proved unexpectantly rewarding because of the shortage in the labor market for computer analysts. As she went for one interview at a major company, she received a call from a friend who asked her to come in for an opening at a major corporation where her friend was employed.

> I decided to go with my friend, which is typical, I think, also a very woman sort of decision. I was a little afraid of a Wall Street Securities corporation because the owner had a reputation of being a slave driver who wanted a fifty, sixty hour week and I had children. So I took a job that was more humane too. I was hoping it would be more concerned with people rather than stocks and bonds, which is interesting enough.

Mrs. Intel's new job was in the Management Information Systems Department at this corporation. It was not the technically advanced environment that she had been used to, in fact, it was a "chaos of computers that didn't communicate with each other. It was a place where computers grew up department by department without an overall total plan. My challege was to get data to go from Radiology, for example, with one kind of system, to Admissions with another kind of system." However, she had a wonderful relationship with her boss, which compensated for the difficulties on the job. Her boss was an engineer from the Soviet Union:

> We did very well together until she unexpectedly became pregnant with her third child and went on maternity leave. There were a lot of people who really felt threatened by her, one above and one below, one wanted her job and another one didn't want her to move up to his job, and they took that opportunity to really play politics. And at that point, my job became bizarre, you know.

Mrs. Intel began to feel very uncomfortable as she also became aware of the bias and discriminatory practices of the "villain," a top level manager who had no real knowledge of computers:

> He used to take all of the reviews for any black employee who was in the department away from their managers who knew their work and write them himself, and they all said, 'slow, low level of knowledge and that sort of stuff.' He told people not to work with them, not to talk to them, not to ask them questions, not to answer their questions, and so on. All this was done in an atmosphere of fear. He created fear, and the only way it came out is when people began to confide and trust in one another a little bit and put together all these stories to see a pattern.

The negative atmosphere on the job intensified, but Mrs. Intel found that getting a new job was difficult, since the whole market was flooded with people coming in. She realized that she needed a college degree in this market; therefore she took this opportunity to leave and go to college. At that time, she also considered changing careers since she had always been interested in or done volunteer work in education. Her work in this corporation also involved teaching: "When I would computerize a new clerical area, training the people to use it was a really enjoyable part of my job. So in a way it helped me to decide to go back to school and go into education for science, technology and math."

Mrs. Intel's husband is an educator and administrator of Adult Education programs. She often helps him at home on the computer with "Lotus and accounting stuff and budgets and grant applications. He is not fond of computers since he is more verbally oriented; he is not a math or music person."

Her older son however, is a computer teacher. "He is a very talented person when it comes to technical things like design and engineering and so on, but he hasn't settled on a career in that area. There is a great demand for computer teachers and he's good at it." He is twenty-five years old and married. Her younger son, who is sixteen, is a good student. He also works in a major hospital as a volunteer.

At the present time, Mrs. Intel is working as an assistant in the Education Department's science lab, while she is completing her coursework. She has four high school interns who help her in the herculean tasks she must complete in twenty hours a week, "which she couldn't possibly do even if she worked forty."

One of her tasks involved the entering of data on the Mac computer. She noticed that while the two boys take to the computer like "ducks to water," the girl says, "I don't want to. I hate computers. I've tried them. All I get is 'syntax error,' 'syntax error,' 'syntax error.'" Mrs. Intel observes:

> While the boys play games, install things, and take chances; the girl is more dutiful. She would want to do a useful, basic program or something. I see this a lot where women and girls don't feel as comfortable just having fun, and they exclude themselves from that type of learning. Months later however, I noticed a new willingness by the young woman to use the computer.

Mrs. Intel attributes her own interest in computers and math to a wonderful math teacher she had in the seventh grade. "He encouraged us to play with math, to really enjoy it and understand it. From then on I really loved it and also different kinds of design." Interestingly, Mrs. Intel was starting to attend a School of Architecture after high school when "family problems, illness, deaths and so on" intervened.

Mrs. Intel originally came to Grant College to develop curricula for science and math and to understand how children learn. She is completing a joint major in the psychology of learning from the Psych Department while taking courses in education. At the present time however, she feels the need to explore more. She explained that there is a need to understand the relationship between teachers and parents in comprehending why students aren't learning science and math. Mrs. Intel expresses her desire for a time of reflection:

> I don't know, I think I'm just going to allow myself, after years and years—before I was a computer programmer I worked in hospitals, I was a clerk. I worked and worked and worked and worked and now I'm just giving myself the luxury I think of going to school and allowing some time for things to germinate before they become useful.

Mrs. Intel concluded the first interview with her thoughts about computers in today's world:

> I think computers are a wonderful tool and I really would like to see people using them. I have a very big problem with thinking of computers as a substitute for teachers, or—I've even heard people in hospitals say they can be a substitute for nurses or the wave of the future, that information is going to replace everything: "We're on

the information super-highway." I think they get too much hype. I mean, I think they're good tools in the hands of intelligent, competent people, and that's it!

## Responses to the Probes and Photographs

### Photograph One

Mrs. Intel stated that she believed there were no differences in computer ability between men and women. She did remember that when she was working with computers she observed that there were differences in style rather than level of knowledge. "Men were more bold and careless, and women were a little more cautious and careful." She also observed in her work with high school interns that boys seemed to have more confidence than girls.

Mrs. Intel stated that she was knowledgeable about biology, chemistry, and computers. She added that she was also knowledgeable about raising children and poetry.

### Photograph Two

Mrs. Intel remembered nothing about her early learning experiences in science, however, she did recall wanting to be a scientist when she was in elementary school. She did not know any scientists but thought it was "the greatest profession." Mrs. Intel stated that the reason she began to study about computers was economics—she needed to make a living for her family. This was a decision that she arrived at on her own since no one in the family had thought of a career in computers.

Mrs. Intel thought that if she had the opportunity to start over again, she would choose a career where she had a great deal of power and influence over the way children were educated. She expressed the desire to be head of the Health, Education and Welfare Department in the government.

### Photograph Three

Mrs. Intel thought that the role of the woman in the photograph was one of the members of a problem solving team.

She described how being a woman had affected her career in the business world: "Frankly it's a liability. One boss told me he doesn't promote women." Another boss told her that women should be at home with the children. However, being a woman proved an asset when she was asked to train women whose clerical jobs were being computerized. "I started with the idea that these were not dumb people who just have to be corraled into learning the computer—but starting with the idea that they were capable people and that they would learn the computer, no problem; it worked." She did not think that being a woman was a liability in education because the atmosphere toward women was more accepting.

## Photograph Four

Mrs. Intel was not sure which of the two women in the photograph she would want to be.

Mrs. Intel recalled her first experience finding a job after completing her coursework in computers. Although it seemed like an eternity, she found a job in a few weeks. Her first boss, who had been a construction worker, gave her challenging assignments on a main frame. Subsequently she has taken courses on using a personal computer and in LAN administration. These courses were given by a private vendor in the city. In her current job as an assistant manager in the science lab she worked with four high school students in a mentoring program. She had encouraged one of the girl interns to use a computer. Mrs. Intel believed that it was helpful for this student to see another woman who worked with computers.

## Photograph Five

Mrs. Intel thought that the woman in the photograph could be a working mother because of the way she was dressed. She said that the woman in the photograph might use the computer after the baby falls asleep.

Mrs. Intel described her home responsibilities. She and her husband shared equally in the job of raising the children and running the home. Her younger son was a very good student who also did volunteer work at a hospital. She recalled he was a little lazy about household chores. Her older son who is now twenty-five and married is moving to Europe. She recalled that he was not very helpful when he was around.

Mrs. Intel said that she used her computer at home in the late evenings. This week she was working until four o'clock in the morning on materials she needed to prepare for the science workshop she was giving for teachers. Mrs. Intel said that it was difficult to concentrate when everyone was at home and her son was usually using the computer for his homework. She found that late evenings were much better for concentration.

## Photograph Six

Mrs. Intel thought that the girl and the boy in the photograph were students or interns. She thought that this was an introductory lesson because the expression on the girl's face was typical of someone who hadn't formulated any questions yet.

Mrs. Intel described the work of three women she knew who use computer based technologies. The first was her former boss who used to be an engineer in the Soviet Union. "If I want to talk technology and what's really happening I talk to Rica." She recalled another friend, Liz, who was a single mother with a teenage daughter. This mother wanted to learn about computers because she wanted to get a computer for her daughter. She wanted her daughter to be computer literate. The third woman was a student in her class who resisted learning to use a computer until she realized it was much easier than typing.

Mrs. Intel described Jane Adams of Hull House as the inspirational woman in her life. She read her autobiography and was very impressed by the concrete way she went about doing things. Mrs. Intel explained that her mother loved her but did not inspire her because she was too passive. She also recalled a sixth grade teacher who was a wonderful inspiration as a social studies teacher. Mrs. Intel stated, "I remember all my teachers, and my fourth-grade teacher especially."

## Photograph Seven

Mrs. Intel expressed mixed reactions to the photograph title "Improving With Age?" She questioned whether things are really progress but she definitely agreed that word processing on the computer was better than typing on the typewriter. She also used the Lotus program to analyze the student's results from a math game when she was an intern. She did correlation's to see the relationship between the student's results on the strategic part and on the mechanical part of the game. She realized that this would have taken months without a computer. She thought that although one can accumulate a great deal of data using a computer, one can also misinterpret the data if you don't know the children.

She considered the computer a tool like a book. There must be planning in the use of computers in schools. Mrs. Intel predicted that in the future girls will encounter computers no matter where they go or what they do. She is concerned however, that while computers are making great changes, the eradication of prejudice against women and minorities will not change unless people work toward that end. She believed that women are going to have to take some risks in confronting these situations and changing them.

## Interview Three

Mrs. Intel suggested one correction, three additions, and one deletion to the six pages of narrative describing her experiences using computer based technologies:

*Correction one*—the word liability should have been the *reliability* was considered important.

*Deletion one*—The name of the first company she worked for.

*Deletion two*—The name of the second company she worked for.

*Addition one*—main frame *assembly language.*

*Addition two—Months later I noticed a new willingness by the young woman to use the computer.*

*Addition three—He (son) works also in research and as a Red Cross volunteer.*

She was shown the transcriptions from interviews' one and two used to develop the narratives. There were 17 transcribed pages for interview one and 37 transcribed pages for interview two.

After I gave a descriptive summary of feminist standpoint theory, I asked her for reactions and or experiences relating to the feminist perspective. Mrs. Intel replied that she rejected the idea that anyone had a monopoly on understanding. She believed feminism emphasized the fact that we are all human beings and can theoretically empathize with other human beings. She believed that most women around the world, whatever their social status or class would react in a similar way to an infant. Mrs. Intel stated that she was a feminist. She realized that there were many feminists who were egomaniacs and showoffs, but there are people like this in any movement. She said that she believed that feminism was necessary and good (Transcript: Interview III, p. 7).

# *Miss Bell*

Miss Bell is an adjunct professor in the Department of Education at Grant College. She is also the tenured principal of an inner city elementary school comprising six hundred children and 30 teachers. Miss Bell is an African American (with Cherokee ancestry on her father's side; her mother's parents came from Barbados), age 45, and divorced.

Miss Bell's first introduction to computers was at the World's Fair in 1964. But her first experience with computers was in 1975, when she held a part time job as a student at Grant College. She taught adults how to read using the computer. Her job was to set up the computer and then work with the person who was learning the language.

The next opportunity she had to learn about computers came through a course that was given at her university in 1978: *Introduction to Computers.* "I was learning some of the programs and that was a little more taxing and a little more frustrating, and we were able to play games and learn some simple procedures."

Almost fifteen years later, after she became principal, she again encountered computers when her school became an A.T.S. school:

> The Automate the Schools Program in the Board of Education meant that all of our attendance-taking, in addition to the attendance books that the teachers had in their classrooms were now entered in the computer and we could generate printouts. We can now find out the percentage of attendance instantly and who is absent. We can also do other information gathering. We can tell exactly how much money we have in all our budgets from the Central Board to the Superintendant's office. And we can follow all our purchase orders from "A" to "Z." We can do ordering also.

Her office in the school also became high tech with a new IBM computer, and laser printer. There were other IBM's in the school; the secretaries used two of them and the assistant principal had one. There was also a fax machine in the outer office.

Miss Bell is very proud of the computer lab in her school which serves students in grades kindergarten through grade six. "Teachers preview the materials first and then coordinate it with what they're teaching in the classroom. We have a library of software and a menu they can choose from." But the computer lab contains the old Commodore computers, third generation computers in need of update to the power of fourth generation programming. The Commodores have been in the school for about ten years. There are also two Macintosh computers in the lab. The lab will be updated as money becomes available.

[Third generation computers emerged with the development of integrated circuits—silicon chips on which thousands of electronic components have been placed together or integrated. Integrated-circuit technology prompted the emergence of the software industry. Standard programs were rewritten to work in contemporary integrated-circuit computers.]

*Computing Concepts*, Duffy and Berchelmann, 1995 (p. 14)

Miss Bell described other computer activities in her school:

Our seniors put together a very nice, if I must brag, yearbook in which they use the word processing end of the computer to produce their yearbook. We have a computer club also. These children actually produce materials for different teachers in different classes. They also can make banners and invitations to different events. I have a fantastic computer teacher and he really coordinates the whole program.

Miss Bell has consulted this computer teacher and her knowledgable assistant principal in her own quest to learn computer based technologies. She had an old Epson computer at home with a monochrome screen. After spending a great deal of time to update this computer with a modem in order to access America Online, she was disappointed at the text display. In her desire to learn more, so that she can help the students in her school to use the information highway, Miss Bell recently purchased a state of the art A.T&.T. computer with modem, fax capabilities, CD-ROM, and sound blaster. She also bought a Canon color printer. Miss Bell is delighted with the color and graphics of the America Online version that she now sees on her new computer.

She devotes several evenings each week to learning about computers with her friend. He works for a private company, and they use computers there. "He talks to these computer experts and then we commiserate about what he found out, like certain codes, and then we use it on his computer or mine." They also search the Internet for grants and other resources that can be accessed for her school.

Miss Bell has two sisters who use computers in their work: "My sister used a computer as a receptionist and secretary working in a law firm. My other sister is also a secretary who works for the Army Corps of Engineers and she uses DOS and Word Perfect. My nephew is also fascinated by the new technology."

Interestingly, Miss Bell also has a palmtop computer which she carries in her purse; it is a Psion:

> It's a handheld one and I keep it in my bag with me, and that's excellent because it sets agendas for you, and it keeps all your phone numbers. It lists everything and has a "to do" list. It does all your basic calculations and school programming. It has an adapter which can be hooked up to a P.C. and can print out and store information. I've just worked with it in the last few months. It will enhance my knowledge and use of the computer at home and school.

Miss Bell has many positive reactions to computer based technologies:

> I think they're great. I know I was a little apprehensive at first, getting into it, because you really don't know what you're doing. But you find out that you really can't break the computer; there's nothing you can do to really hurt it. And it can help you. It's really fantastic. I'm mesmerized when I travel by plane and I see other women just whip out their laptops, and they're typing away and getting things done. I'm sitting there maybe reading a book, you know, and it delays, but they're so productive, and that fascinates me. I think it's one of the greatest inventions. I could see a lot of future use, and I want to get into computers, into the super-highway, the informational highway. That's my goal, to learn more and more about it.

Miss Bell also shared some negative effects of computer based technologies in her role as an educator:

> Parents have to be aware and educators too. We don't have too much of a problem because we're not that well equiped yet in the school, but at home, children have to know that there is value in going to a library and accessing a book rather than just using a computer. There's something to being socialized with other kids in these activities. I mean kids of your own age and things like that and communicating. You need to communicate with human beings and not just be isolated with a computer someplace in your room or house. Two parents were saying that their children are a little bit lazy about going to a library because they could just press a button and there's the information: the encyclopedia comes up with the material. They ought to know the process of going to get a book and the value of reading a book.

Miss Bell's vision for herself and the youngsters she supervises is future-oriented with unlimited possibilities in computer based technolgies:

> I think it's going to be fantastic if we keep moving at the pace we're moving now with computers. This little girl (in photograph seven) will be able to stand on the beach, which is very symbolic, and look up into the skies and communicate with someone on another planet. Yes, I think that and we will have that kind of technology in twenty-five years.

## Responses to the Probes and Photographs

### Photograph One

Miss Bell stated that women and men are equally knowledgeable about computers. She believed that computer ability had nothing to do with gender but with an individual's ability. She thought that women were more intuitive than men because their intuition is more developed. She thought that women socialize better with other women and men seem to want to socialize with women because they feel more comfortable talking to women about deep situations and topics.

She believed that she was more knowledgeable about social studies and education. Miss Bell thought that she was more intuitively oriented. "I do listen to that inner voice, and it never leads me wrong." She stated that when she worked on computer programs that were unfamiliar and the instructions were not clear she was able through intuition to arrive at where she was going

### Photograph Two

Miss Bell recalled her early learning experiences in science. She thought that she was fortunate to have science teachers who did a great deal of experimentation and hands on learning. They also emphasized critical thinking and deductive reasoning.

Miss Bell wanted to be an elementary school teacher from the age of eight. But she believed that her present job of principal was something she was supposed to be doing. Her former boss, who was her principal, and her superintendent were instrumental in motivating her to apply for the position. She stated that she enjoyed college teaching but it was not something that she would have chosen first.

## Photograph Three

Miss Bell thought that the woman in the photograph was an expert who was helping the men with a computer program. Miss Bell indicated that she had worked with computers as part of a job at Grant College when she was a student.

Miss Bell stated that being a woman was initially the reason she was appointed principal. The district wanted to hire a woman because of the affirmative action degree. However, she found that once on the job she had to prove herself because other women and men did not take her leadership role seriously. She believed that people expect men to be leaders.

## Photograph Four

Miss Bell chose the woman in yellow in the photograph as the woman she would like to be because "her face seems to show that she's intrigued or interested in her work." Miss Bell thought that the computer was a great time-saver and the information highway allowed access to all kinds of learning expereinces. She described her ability to obtain and store information on her hand held computer.

Miss Bell's introduction to computers in college was in the late '70's. She enrolled in a course that involved a great deal of game-playing on the computer. She was not able to adapt the computer to her work as a student but as a principal she recognized it as an invaluable tool. Her school has an ATS system, Automate the Schools Program, that gathers information on attendance. She can also access information on other financial matters relating to the school's budget.

Miss Bell purchased a state of the art AT&T computer with a modem, CD-ROM, and sound card. She described the many programs that came pre-installed on her computer. Miss Bell was able to access the Internet on this new computer with her friend Juan. They share information that he learns from computer networking on his job. When she was asked what her collegues think of her computer skills she replied, "I don't talk a lot, so they don't react too much." Her nephew and her sister are fascinated by the new technology.

## Photograph Five

Miss Bell thought that the woman in the photograph appeared to be a working mother because of the way she was dressed. "She's dressed as if she has just come from the world of business." Miss Bell described her responsibilities that she shared with her sister as a landlord. "She does some of the work I am not able to do—that's keeping up the outer parts of the house like the garden and the backyard." She and her sister share a two-family home.

Miss Bell described the use of the computer on the job. She had many computer files that she would use regularly. For example she would find a computer file with a letter to the parents in her school and update it. She indicated that this saved time and work for her secretary. Her school day began at seven o'clock and continued until nine o'clock at night. She also worked at the school in the evening as an adjunct instructor. Her elementary school students and parents would join the Grant College students in learning about social studies.

She also attended district office meetings and was active on the recruitment team to find qualified teachers for the district. She is also part of the Curriculum team. Her school has been designated a Comer school which means there are many meetings to attend on all levels.

## Photograph Six

Miss Bell thought that the woman in the photograph was the supervisor and she was anxiously waiting for some information to be accessed through the young woman. She thought that the supervisor was not happy with the information she was getting.

Miss Bell described many women in her family who used computers. Her aunt, who was a college professor and her daughter who was a computer analyst lived in another state but communicated by phone. Miss Bell's sister Karen worked for the Army and used computers in her work.

She said that her stepmother was the woman who inspired her the most. She was a positive role model during her childhood. Miss Bell said she was a strong person who had gone to business and then became a housewife. She would always take on projects and do things extravagantly.

Her computer goal was to chat with educators on-line and find information related to grants and funding for her school.

## Photograph Seven

Miss Bell had mixed reaction to the photograph title "Improving with Age?" She said there was no comparison between a typewriter and the CD-ROM. But she cautioned that parents have to be aware that the computer can be addictive. She thought that children should be taught the value of accessing a library book and socializing with other children.

Miss Bell predicted that if we keep moving at the pace we are moving one day a little girl will be able to stand on a beach and use the computer to communicate with someone on another planet. She said that even now girls have been given more choices. Miss Bell believed that if a girl had the ability she would have the same opportunity to do whatever she wants to do because the information will be at her fingertips.

### Interview Three

Miss Bell suggested two corrections, one addition and no deletions to the five pages of narrative describing her experiences with computer based technologies.

*Correction one*—Cherokee ancestry on her *father's* side.

*Correction two*—Single to *divorced*.

*Addition one*—Mother's parents were from Barbados.

She was shown the transcriptions from interviews one and two used to develop the narrative. There were 17 pages from interviews' one and 31 pages from interview two.

After I gave a descriptive summary of feminist standpoint theory I asked Miss Bell for reactions and experiences relating to the feminist perspective. Miss Bell stated that she did not consider herself a feminist. She did not believe in taking part in any extreme groups. She was a human being who happened to be female. She believed that there were differences between males and females in outlook but it was important to understand that people were people. She emphasized the need to live together as an educational community. She did not like to segregate herself in any manner (Transcript: Interview III, p. 4, 5/6/95).

## *Dr. Goldman*

Dr. Goldman is an assistant professor and director of the puppetry center at Grant College. She is also a home-bound teacher for the Board of Education for twenty-two years. Dr. Goldman is a European American, age 53, married and the mother of two children: one son and one daughter.

Dr. Goldman, who earned her Ed.D. from a major university in the eastern part of the United States, described her initial learning experience with computers:

My first reaction to the fact that I had to use a computer was a bit of panic. I don't like machines, although I had perfect confidence in my abilities to learn a language, even a difficult language like Chinese, in a few months. But, I panic sometimes when my answering machine doesn't work or when I can't get the alarm to work. I started with the computer sort of cautiously. I took a course at Grant College in adult education about a year ago. I was busy and missed a few sessions, but I basically learned to shut the computer on and off and so on. And then I got out a book and worked with a friend, and I was able to use the computer as a sort of advanced typewriter. I didn't make much effort to understand the functions of the different parts. I just wanted to make it do what I wanted it to do. And I found that I loved it.

Dr. Goldman's interest in the computer was intensified when she realized that it was possible to print flyers, and develop booklets for her center. She hired a college student to help her design the graphics and page layout for the textbook that she was writing on whole language activities. But this proved to be very expensive, so she decided to put the first draft on the computer herself. Dr. Goldman recently purchased a state of the art fourth generation Macintosh computer complete with CD-ROM, multimedia, scanner, and printer.

[Fourth generation computers replace magnetic-core memory by silicon-chip memory and place much more circuitry on each chip. The microprocessor was created which was a single chip containing all the circuitry required to make it programmable. Today, LSI (large scale integration) and VLSI (very large-scale integration) technology enables hundreds of thousands of electronic components to be stored on one chip. Using VLSI, a manufacturer can make a small computer that rivals the power of a room-sized first-generation computer.]
*Computing Concepts,* Duffy and Berchelmann, 1995, (p. 16)

Dr. Goldman has used her computer to access information on funding and grants for her puppet center, but that is not her ultimate goal:

I learned a little about the Internet, and I figured, well why not? I love to visit with people from other countries, and the thought of being able to access library files without having to go out in the cold, being able to take a nice hot cup of coffee and a pickle and sit next to my computer and talk to people in Israel, Brazil, Puerto Rico—I find that absolutely incredible.

Now, however, she is faxing stories and songs that she has edited on her computer. She is sharing these projects with educators in Brazil, Puerto Rico and Israel. She is also experimenting with the possibility of editing background music for her projects using the CD-ROM. Dr. Goldman is continuously developing materials to use in her teaching about culture and language.

Dr. Goldman thinks that her present career was influenced by the Hebrew studies that she was involved in while at a Yeshiva and later in seminary. These studies were in ancient Hebrew and linguistics, which developed a love for words and language. She uses her puppets as a tool for teaching about language. Dr. Goldman cannot recall the earlier experiences that might have influenced her career because she was involved in a car accident when she was twenty two which left her with epileptic seizures for ten years with accompanying loss of early childhood memories. She has since recovered from these seizures but recounts one of many "funny incidents": "I was giving a birthday party for my daughter and I had a seizure, and when I woke up I explained to the kids that it was an illness."

Dr. Goldman works with homebound children in the morning and in the afternoon she is in charge of five high school students engaged in a fieldwork assignment. At the college, she teaches courses in language arts and reading. Every other spare moment is devoted to her center activities. She has hired two actors, puppeteers, who give performances at elementary schools. She works with them on constructing, producing and directing the presentation. Teachers also come to the center for workshops in interdisciplinary curriculum planning. Dr. Goldman uses her Power Book, a lap-top at the center and her Mac at home.

> I like to put on my pajamas and take my salad and coffee downstairs, and if I'm working on a project, I like to take my time with it or discuss it with someone on the phone. I can do this at the same time that I am cooking supper.

Dr. Goldman has two for supper each night; her husband and her daughter. Her husband is a retired teacher who uses the computer system in the travel agency he works in. When I asked if he was involved with her home computer, she responded, "No, he's involved to the extent that he's a little nervous that I'll invite the people home that I talk to on the Internet." Dr. Goldman has opened her home to many visitors in her travels. Interestingly, Dr. Goldman considers the computer "someone she is getting to know personally."

> I guess you can say it's like a child or a spouse: It's company, It's someone to talk to and work with, and it doesn't always do what I ask it to do. I think I'll name it Wilbur. I'm not sure quite why, but it's not a female. It's not cooperative enough.

Dr. Goldman has reservations about the use of the computer in today's society.

> I hesitate even to say it, because it sounds very old fashioned to say, I'm thinking back to the good old days, but the fact is that kids are sedentary. There's something to be said for roller skating and hopscotch, and all the games you play. I think kids read more today. The computer is a very easy way to alleviate boredom, and if kids never get bored, they never look for interesting things to do. On the other hand, you could say that the computer is a way to use thinking skills, and kids can interact with it and develop mentally. But it is very sedentary.

Dr. Goldman notes the possibility of a future class division of our society by those who are computer literate and those who are not:

> I think that one of the effects of computer technology will be that it creates more of an upper class and a lower class; in other words, there are less jobs that require low skill, and there is a lot of competition for the jobs requiring technology. This little girl (in photograph seven) will either have to become a part of the technological age or live a difficult life. There won't be much in the way of the simple life any more.

## Responses to the Probes and Photographs

### Photograph One

Dr. Goldman expressed the belief that men are more knowledgeable about computers than women. Then, she qualified her answer and added that it depended on age. "Middle-age women in my generation have been doing other things. We've been more involved in things outside of work. Whereas men are at work for longer hours and have gotten into the computer age a bit more."

Dr. Goldman believed that she was most knowledgeable about English, and Language Arts.

Dr. Goldman thought that women and men were intuitive to the same degree. She said that she usually is guided by her instincts. In fact, she resisted learning about the computer until she realized it could help her communicate with other people through the Internet. She stated that she was not interested in how the computer works but in what it could do to help her in her center.

## Photograph Two

Dr. Goldman stated that she did not remember anything about learning science in elementary school. However, she did remember dissecting a frog in junior high school.

Dr. Goldman said that when she was little she wanted to be a wanderer and travel around the world. She believed that this idea originated in her Hebrew studies at the yeshiva. She was involved in Biblical studies, ancient Hebrew, and linguistics. She was interested in words and language as a child at the yeshiva and later in her studies at the seminary. She indicated that her work at the puppet center demonstrated the use of puppets as a tool for teaching language.

## Photograph Three

Dr. Goldman suggested that the woman in the photograph was someone the men were trying to teach the computer to unsuccessfully. She thought that the woman might be a technician, a secretary, or a teacher.

## Photograph Four

Dr. Goldman did not choose to be either women in the photograph because she did not want to work at a job just using the computer. She wanted to work with people. She stated that she appreciated what the computer could do because she has used it for publishing at her center. She did not speak to her colleagues or friends about her computer skills. "No. In other words, it's just something that I am doing.

## Photograph Five

Dr. Goldman thought that the woman in the photograph was a working mother because her husband was watching television and she was nicely dressed. She stated that the woman in the photograph used the computer at night when she came home from work or she wondered if the woman had a home-based job.

Dr. Goldman described her home responsibilities as cooking and the general care of the home and family. She also worked full time in her job teaching home bound children and at the puppet center. Her work at the puppet center consisted of directing many projects and the offshoots from them. She was involved in grant writing, publishing materials, and keeping track of the employees at the center. She indicated that her husband was retired and did the bulk of the housework. She did the cooking and shopping and he did everything else.

## Photograph Six

Dr. Goldman thought that the woman in the photograph was a teacher who was working with a student. She was showing her how to enter data on the computer for a research study. The teacher was trying to see if the student understood what she was doing.

Dr. Goldman indicated that she knew only two women who used computers. She named this researcher and a teacher. She could not think of a third women who used computer based technologies.

Dr. Goldman said that the most inspirational woman she knew was her mother who was also a fantastic teacher. She taught in the public schools and part time at the yeshiva in the English Department. Dr. Goldman was also a student at this yeshiva. She stated that she was not sent there because of religious reasons but that Jewish children of her generation were sent there to study for cultural reasons.

## Photograph Seven

Dr. Goldman had mixed reactions to the photograph title "Improving With Age?" She thought the computer was a fantastic improvement over the typewriter. But she considered the style of life that goes with the computer age not necessarily an improvement. She said that the computer has helped to reach children with learning disabilities or learning a language because the computer is interesting to children. However, she thought that children who use computers do not engage in sports or interact with other children. She believed the computer games were addictive to children.

Dr. Goldman predicted that computer based technology will create more of an upper class and lower class because there will be a great deal of competition for jobs requiring technology. Girls who are not computer literate will lead a difficult life. She thought that living in the future will no longer be simple or uncomplicated. She did predict that computer technology will benefit girls who are computer literate by giving them more occupational choices. She believed that computer learning will begin in kindergarten.

Dr. Goldman did not believe that the computer would replace a teacher because of the human factor. "The human factor is always the significant factor and computers have no emotion. Most of the things that influence us are emotional connections."

Dr. Goldman also indicated that she had been in a car accident when she was twenty years old. This accident erased many of the memories of her childhood.

### Interview Three

Dr. Goldman suggested one correction, no additions and no deletions to the five pages of narrative describing her experiences using computer based technologies:

*Correction one—Ed.D.* in place of Ph.D.

She was shown the transcriptions from interviews' one and two used to develop the narrative. There were 12 transcribed pages from interview one and 21 pages from interview two.

After I gave a descriptive summary of feminist standpoint theory, I asked her for reactions and or experiences relating to the feminist perspective. Dr. Goldman stated that she had thought that feminism had produced some very positive changes in our society but that it went too far. She believed that men and women should receive equal pay for the same work and that women should not be excluded from any of the jobs that men do. But she thought that women need a certain amount of protection. She did not want to open her own car doors and she wanted the compliments and perks that go with being a woman. She also believed that a woman in authority can use her feminine personality and ability to create a work force where the workers are highly motivated, enthusiastic, and have high morale. She believed that feminism had gone too far and women have had to be responsible for two jobs instead of one. She believed even the sexual revolution had gone too far.

Dr. Goldman described her experience with workers who were asked to give her an estimate on the repairs to her house. "Someone comes and quotes me a price and invariably it's higher than if they talk to my husband." She believed that this type of attitude still exists in society. She thought that feminism has helped a great deal in the workforce.

# *Miss Lee*

Miss Lee is a newly appointed elementary school teacher. She is an Asian American, age 24, and single. Her parents came from China. Miss Lee's initial experience with computers began in the sixth grade; she attended a computer science course where she learned to scroll her name across the computer screen:

> It was more of a computer programming course. It was hard for the teacher to do the course also: It was the first year the computers were in the school. They were big black and grey boxes, RCA ones. They were pretty old, considering now. It was a course that we went to on a prep for my teacher. We went to this room and there were six computers, but it was still a class of thirty or so children. It was six to a computer, so you got your turn. It wasn't windows, no mouse, nothing. It was keyboard and it was a lot of fun. I'm sure we learned other things, but the thing that stands out, cause it was the most fun, that we actually got to scroll across the screen. That was pretty neat for an eleven or twelve year old.

Many years later, she enrolled in a computer course in college where she was a business major. The course was for beginners and was supposed to give students experience in keyboarding and using the Internet.

> Actually in order to pass the course you had to type a paper, any paper you wanted to, even for another course. The professor just wanted to see if you could apply the different skills that we learned in class, whether it was formatting or doing spreadsheets or even a bank checking account.

Miss Lee subsequently changed majors from business to education and enrolled in Grant College. When asked why, she responded:

> I didn't see it as fun any more to have economics class after economics class after political science class. And then I couldn't even picture myself sitting in an office for the rest of my life. I just happened to land in education by accident but ended up loving it. I took a summer job working with some kids at a camp, and then I took courses, because I didn't want to stop going to school. I knew if I stopped, I would never start again. So I took some courses and ended up in education.

Miss Lee was still interested in learning about computers because "I knew it was going to be the thing of the future." She enrolled in a desktop-publishing course at Grant College, where she had to create a children's book using Pagemaker:

> In this course I found that out of twenty-five or thirty females, maybe five or six of us actually got through this course legitimately. We didn't ask our boyfriends to come and do the program, or come and work on this for us, or had our friends do it. I thought it was funny that I didn't find out that until the end of the year that some people said, "I do have a 'B' and I can't believe it. I didn't even do that paper." It was frustrating, but funny also, because it was that female syndrome, I guess. Just looking back, you know, they were going to do it to those computers. I don't know what the real problem was, actually; I don't know if it was computers or because they were just the type of the people that they were, that it could have been any project and somebody else would have done it for them.

Miss Lee remembered the book that she had written. It was based on an African folktale, "Ananci and The Moss-Covered Rock." She had to retell it and illustrate the story using a scanning device to copy the pictures and design the layout. "I really enjoyed that class."

Miss Lee's initial experience with the computer was challenging:

> I remember the first few days being very frustrated and not being able to follow. It was frustrating. But after a while you get the hang of it and I took chances opening different windows. You had to really play around before you get a feel for what's in there, because if I didn't open it up, I never would have found, "Oh, I could try this one, and if it's wrong then it's wrong." But I had it saved on a disk, so I could alsways go back. I thought that I did a lot of risk-taking for that course: It was twenty-five to one or thirty to one; it was thirty females to one because the professor had his assistant teach the course. The professor and his assistant were males. "Yes, funny. So you had to work on your own and take a chance and 'psst' next to you, 'Do you think I should do this?' And "How did you get that?' It was that kind of course."

She developed her skills on the Macintosh as a result of that course, which helped her to obtain a job in the Education office. Miss Lee indicated that she does not have a computer at home, only a word processor, because, "We don't have the space or the money for a computer."

We don't have one at home, but my uncle studied and graduated as a computer programmer, so that's the only one who used a computer. But I haven't really got into talking to him about computers. I'm not one to talk about it.

Miss Lee just completed her undergraduate studies in elementary education and sociology. She is at present an early childhood teacher in an elementary school but most of her children are from another neighborhood.

They're all from the apartment buildings, and I have the overcrowded situation. It's a lot of children and they don't speak English. I have a lot of Pakistaniis, Indians, and Hispanics. And one or two Asians. That's my mix of children.

Miss Lee would love to have computer in her classroom for the children, but she does not even have access to a computer for her own use in the school.

I think it would be wonderful for them to have that chance, being especially the children that I work with, where they probably don't even know what a computer is nor have ever seen a typewriter, never mind a computer. The one thing I found fascinating with my kids is that they come in and talk about Segogenesis and Supersonic Knuckles. These are computer games. I have one or two boys that have access to computers, or even know the computer games, which is funny.

Miss Lee recalled her earlier computer goal at college where she hoped to access the Internet:

Oh, that I can call a total failure, I guess. I am still not familiar with the Internet and it is frustrating. I got as far as sending E-mail messages to the teaching assistant and he sent me messages back. I couln't even get to talk to anybody in Australia or whatever he had us hooked up to. I couldn't figure it out even after a whole semester. No one helped me because it was a very crowded kind of class and time didn't allow. At this college, the business classes were at minimum fifty. I had lectures where I sat in a lecture hall with five hundred and seventy-five other people. I wasn't interested in it after a while. When I got into the course, I really wanted to learn the Internet, but it was overwhelming. I lost interest after a while I guess. I took it with my roommate, and at that point it became the biggest joke. It was 'Let's go type our paper.' But I think if I sat down and had more time, now I think I have more patience, and I am more comfortable with sitting in front of the computer and taking the chance of opening this and pressing that.

When Miss Lee was a little girl, her dream was to be a gold medalist in skating at the Olympics. Today she whirls through a day of teaching, taking courses, and giving workshops to teachers in science education. Her day does not end, however, until she cleans the house and prepares dinner for her two sisters, one brother, grandfather and mother who works late. "The pace is killing me. But it's been fun. A lotta hard work."

## Responses to the Probes and Photographs

### Photograph One

Miss Lee stated that women weren't given as many opportunities to use a computer, therefore some women are less knowledgeable than men. She believed that women were more familiar with life experiences and not technical subjects such as computers. She thought women were pushed into more maternal things.

Miss Lee considered herself more knowledgeable in science and math. She believed in women's intuition which she said she used to explore unfamiliar programs and software on the computer. "Right, there's no logic behind it; it's just, 'Well, I'm never gonna find out unless I try it.' So—I do try it."

### Photograph Two

Miss Lee recalled her early learning experiences in elementary school science. "It was a lot of just listening and looking in textbooks and learning from books, never this show-and-tell, so to speak, so I see here in this picture." Miss Lee noted that the boy was holding the frog and the girls looked "squeamish" in the photograph. She indicated that this would not happen if gender stereotyping had not made children do "boy" things and "girl" things.

When Miss Lee was little she wanted to be a gold medalist in roller skating. She also wanted to be a teacher because of her first grade teacher. The fondest memory she recalled was in that grade because her teacher was a very nice woman who really cared for the children.

## Photograph Three

Miss Lee suggested that the woman in the photograph was probably someone who was supposed to type something and "screwed it up." She thought that the men were very upset because of this situation.

Miss Lee recalled her first job working on a computer in the science lab in the Education Department. She believed it was not gender discrimination that she was experiencing in her present job but age discrimination. She was frustrated by the attitude toward young teachers. "Young teachers are not appreciated and they do not expect as much from you." This attitude was very different from her job in the science lab where the person she worked for expected her to do whatever the job entailed including the lifting of heavy boxes.

## Photograph Four

Miss Lee decided that she would like to be the woman in the photograph who was working alone in the office. She thought the woman showed more confidence because she worked alone. However, the other woman seemed as if she needed help because someone was watching her.

She believed that computers were the technology of the future and that motivated her to start learning. At Grant College she enrolled in a course in creative arts and literature where she had to write a story and produce it on the computer. After this experience she has said, "Computers can do wonders, let me learn more."

## Photograph Five

Miss Lee thought the woman in the photograph was not a working mother because she was not ambitious enough. Then she decided that the woman may have come home from work because the husband was already sitting at home. She wondered if he was a house husband.

She thought the woman in the photograph might use the computer at night to manage the family money, by budgeting and then banking it.

Miss Lee described her work experiences. She taught a kindergarten class all day and then she came home to help prepare the family dinner. Her mother worked late and as the oldest child in the house it was her responsibility to help with household chores. Her grandfather also helped to get the dinner started because he was home all day. Several evenings a week she also taught science workshops to elementary school teachers at Grant College.

## *Photograph Six*

Miss Lee thought that the photograph portrayed a class in the computer lab. She thought that the woman was the computer teacher and that the young man and young woman were her students.

Miss Lee was asked to described three women whom she knew who use computers. She mentioned her sister and the school secretary, but she could not think of a third woman. "And another woman. That's a tough one [pauses]. Another woman."

Miss Lee chose her mother as the inspirational woman in her life. Although her mother was not an educated woman she was a hard working and determined woman who cared for her family. She worked in a factory as a seamstress. Miss Lee recalled that she had great physical and emotional strength. "She was strong and she respected us. She depended on us as we depended on her. But you knew when not to push your luck."

## *Photograph Seven*

Miss Lee had mixed reactions to the photograph title "Improving with Age?" She believed that we were more advanced because of computers and that things that were done on the computer were much faster. But she thought that life was more complicated now and more difficult. There was so much more to learn. "Computers have made things happen faster, made things happen more extraordinarily, picture-wise, color-wise, and it's fascinating."

Miss Lee reflected that as an educator she found it very difficult to teach computer skills. She thought that children should learn by playing on the computer and trying ideas out. She indicated that she had learned computer skills that way. Miss Lee believed that although children are playing games, they are getting the experience they need to help them advance later when they will eventually learn how to use computer programs.

Miss Lee predicted that women in the future will be able to work from home on a computer smaller than a briefcase. "She'll probably be able to do the family thing—be a mother, yet also work as a businesswoman, because that's how advanced we'll be with faxes and the computer and telecommunications."

Miss Lee believed that a computer would never replace a teacher because of the emotional support a teacher can give.

*Interview Three*

Miss Lee suggested one correction, one addition, and no deletions to the five pages of narrative describing her experiences using computer based technologies:

*Correction one*—undergraduate studies in elementary education and sociology.

*Addition one*—Parents are from Canton in China.

She was shown the transcriptions from interviews' one and two used to develop the narrative. There were 16 pages from interview one and 24 pages from interview two.

After I gave a descriptive summary of feminist standpoint theory, I asked her for reactions and or experiences relating to the feminist perspective.

Miss Lee stated that she thought it was wonderful that women tried to encourage each other to stand up for their rights. She said that she had feminist ideals but that she did not think she was a true feminist because she was not politically involved. She also said that some feminists are hypocritical and want the rights that men have but they want the standards lowered. She believed that some feminists forget that women have limitations that are physical and cultural. She thought that women are different and should be treated differently than men.

# Mrs. Standish

Mrs. Standish is an appointed elementary school teacher in this city. She has taught five years and is now on childcare leave. Mrs. Standish is 31 years old, married, and the mother of two sons: Harry, age 2 1/2 and Daniel, age 1.

Mrs. Standish's earliest memory of computer use goes back to the sixth or seventh grade in a middle school in the southern part of the United States.

> I remember the school got a computer, and it was a very big deal, and it was a large thing, and it was housed in a large closet. There was a modem. I don't know if it was a modem that we use today, but it was a modem. It was hooked up through a telephone line and it was a big clunky thing. I was very fascinated, very curious as to what it really did, and I think it we put in some information, and it printed up something. That was my earliest memory.

Many years later, she again encountered computers while attending college in another state.

> I was an international business and Spanish major. They had a computer lab in the Economics Depatment that nobody used and I would go there to type my papers. I remember going in there one evening and there were all boys there, I was the only girl. They were all computer nerds with calculators hanging off their belts. You know, the stereotypical computer nerd. I remember sitting down and being a little nervous about the whole thing, but I just politely asked the fellow next to me questions to help me along, and he was very nice and got me going. And then with science classes I would do the same, and it always seemed there were more men than women using the computers. But everybody was always really friendly and helpful, and basically once you get comfortable, the computer sort of tells you what to do.

When Mrs. Standish was a child, she wanted to be a baton twirler, and then a teacher, and later a marine biologist. She described the reason for her career change from investment banking to education.

> My college friend and I moved to New York City together. I was working in investment banking and I was very unhappy with my work. It was not what I wanted to do. It was sort of helping the rich get richer and I felt that I wasn't doing anything productive for our society, I was helping people that really didn't need help. Their objective for the day was to make "x" amount of dollars and that turned me off. Everybody I worked with was very superficial and wanted to earn money, and that was it. I was about to leave, when somebody tried to pull me into the computer part of this corporation, and I said I'm not interested and left.

> In the banking world, people have a tendency to see you as a woman initially, and make negative judgments right away. But I think there's a tendency to just sort of size you up and say, 'Oh, she's a woman; she has these capabilities; she'll go this far and not further. They predetermine how far you can go in the company. My first boss, who was involved in technical forecasting for a bank, hired me to market his business and run his subscription service. He gave me a lot of responsibility, but he was condescending in the way he treated me in meetings with other people. He would blame things on me, that were not my responsibility; they were his responsibility. He also promised me a percentage of the growth of the business, from

the point I came in. He didn't deliver on any of his promises. I think he felt that he could get away with it because I was a woman. He would give me jewelry like little earrings or a pearl necklace. It was never near the value of what I contributed and what they promised me, so I left.

My college friend, who lived in the same building in this city, was teaching in the public schools. She said, "Why don't you come teach; you would be great." I had always thought about teaching. She told me the Board of Education has emergency certification and would hire me if I passed a few simple tests and had a B.A. I would only have a year's contract and I didn't have to worry about committing to somebody for a long time. I tried it out and I really loved it. Then I signed a contract saying I would get my Master's in a certain amount of time. So I stuck with teaching.

Although Mrs. Standish's first school did not have computers, her second school "had a ton of them."

It was a Chapter One school, and it served the Projects which were on one side of the school and a nicer neighborhood which was on the other side. The Principal's strength was writing grants and getting money; her school had the best supplies, from computers to books in the district. She also had a museum in the school, and in the museum was a computer for teachers to use. It had a CD-ROM and encyclopedia on the computer. It was terrific.

I would also take my students into the computer lab and help them. The programs that were run were workbook-type programs. The school also had a writing-to-read lab for kindergarteners and first graders. I taught a fourth grade so my class never used that lab.

Mrs. Standish also had opportunities to learn about computers in Grant College while going for her master's degree.

I had a terrific experience with Logo, which is for older kids. Ever since I took that course I've wanted to take it back to school, but I haven't taught since I took that course. So I'm really anxious to bring that knowledge back with me because it's going to open doors for children in math that would normally be scared of math, because it teaches children math without them realizing it. The course was a little scary, just like anything, because the professor gave us few instructions. And that's how you learned: You learned by actually having to figure out how to move the cursor which is called a "turtle." Eventually I drew elaborate pictures, but first it was trying to figure out how to make a square, and other shapes. And that was very intriguing. I love that program.

My husband, who is an architect, is very into math. I let him read the book on Logo by Seymour Papert. He was very intrigued by it because this fellow learned math through an Erector set, and that's how my husband learned math.

Mrs. Standish believed that the world has been more opened to boys because of their early childhood experiences, but she believed that computers will make a difference:

But with computers, I think more girls have more access to computers than they did to toys in my age growing up. I think it's going to be real interesting to see boys and girls take these programs and just take off, because I think girls are just as capable as boys are in the world of mathematics and science.

Mrs. Standish reflected on her early school experiences that developed an interest in math. "I think that when I started taking math in school I did well, and that gave me confidence in that area." However, Mrs Standish's school experiences were unusual. Since her father was a professional athlete, she started out in the Midwest and then moved to the coast. She attended a Montessori school there. Then she moved back to the Midwest and then on down to the southern part of the United States.

The whole family went with him as he moved. Toward the end, we went out when he transferred to another team for two seasons, back and forth. Then later when he was transferred to this team; we didn't move but we would travel to the games. My mom thought it was very important to go to his games. Then when he finished and started coaching, we all moved down South. There were four of us.

My younger brother and I didn't really get the gifts, but I played field hockey and lacrosse, and I swam competitively. I started swimming competitively when I was in first grade and I stopped when I was in high school.

Mrs. Standish believed that her childhood experiences of moving and meeting new people helped her to adapt to changes later in life. One of these changes involved the computer that she had bought:

> When he first opened his office, my husband was working out of our home in the front room. He took over the computer with his business, and then he moved his business out of the home and stole the computer in the last year. So we haven't had a computer at home when I desperately needed it for school. It was an IBM. So I had to go to his office to use it for typing papers. But, we've been meaning to buy a multimedia P.C. for the home and any day now we are going to get one. We just bought the other side of our house, so we have to wait until we get a little more money back in savings.

Mrs. Standish is very excited about getting a Multimedia P.C. because "the sky's the limit with a Multimedia computer." She has definite computer goals:

> I want to access the Internet. There's a teacher' network that I would like to plug into. I was plugged into that at P.S. 702 when I left, and then I went to another school, my last school, and they don't have any computers with modems. And then, you know, a CD-ROM: I am very excited that my children growing up will be able to have an encyclopedia on the CD with all of the pictures that they can get, the live pictures, the voice, the sounds they can hear. They can hear J.F.K's voice when they plug into the computer.

Mrs. Standish's computer ability extends beyond wordprocessing and telecommunications. She is actively involved in the business part of her husband's architectural practice:

> Well, since I finished school, I've started going into his office one day a week, because he's drowning in paperwork and administrative stuff. I have been working on spreadsheets with the computer doing his expenses and billing. I use Microsoft Excel for Windows.

Mrs. Standish intends to go back to teaching, but she is not ready to leave her infant yet. She recalls that she was pregnant with him in school and was still in school when she had him. "I'm thinking it would be really appealing to be at home with the younger one and have special time with him three days a week, since he didn't have the start that Harry did." She feels that the ideal situation would be to start back to work as a teacher when both children are in kindergarten, so that they can all have the same schedule. Interestingly, her desire to go back to school involves more than financial reasons:

> I had a special opportunity to work for Mr. Smith before he died. He was the principal that went to the Projects to look for a student and then was shot. He got caught in the crossfire, and I was on leave at the time. Of course, I was very disturbed by the the whole thing. About a month  or two later, I had a dream, and he came to me in this dream, and I said, "Mr. Smith, what're you doing here? You're dead." He said, "I know, but I just wanted to come back and tell you that I'm at peace and everything is okay and that I want you to return to my school and I want you to do something very specific." He said, "I want you to go back there and get the computer lab back together," because the computer lab was dismantled when I first went, because the teacher went on sabbatical, and so they separated all the computers and put one in each classroom. Teachers really don't use these computers because they feel intimidated and really don't know what to do. He said he wanted me to go back, get the lab back together, get more computers in the school, because he felt that those students would not have a chance in the world without computer skills, and I needed to take care of that.

> In the morning, when I awoke, and remembered my dream, I felt a little weird, felt a little spooky, but at the same time it felt very comfortable and I felt that he really did come to me and tell me that I needed to do this.

Mrs. Standish thinks that computers are an "incredible" educational tool, but she realizes that there are negatives:

> I think it depends on the programs that are used in schools. I hear teachers talking about how scared they are that it might replace them, and I don't think a computer could ever replace a teacher. I think programs like workbook-type programs are pretty superficial, and they certainly can't replace a teacher. It's sort of busy work and I think that can be dangerous. Schools and teachers have to watch out and not get the children plugged into those types of programs for good. In programs like Logo, programming programs, children can teach themselves and go at their own pace, and just learn so much and really gain a lot of confidence throughout the process.

## Responses to the Probes and Photographs

### Photograph One

Mrs. Standish thought that people who were starting to learn about computers when they were older feel awkward whereas children who begin to learn about computers when they are very young do not. She also stated that she believed that women find it easier to learn about computers when they are older than men because women's egos are not as easily damaged as men's egos are. She thought that women are more open to learning new things. However, she believed that both men and women are both knowledgeable about computers once they have started learning.

Mrs. Standish believed that she was knowledgeable in math and science. She said that she has a sixth sense about many things which she calls her intuition. But she believes her logical reasoning, not her intuition, has helped her to learn about computer based technologies.

### Photograph Two

Mrs. Standish recalled her early learning experiences in elementary school. She remembered science lessons that involved inventing things in the fifth grade in a school in the South.

When she was little she wanted to be a baton twirler. Then she wanted to be a teacher and after that a scientist. If she had a second choice today she would like to be a politician so that she could effect change in public policy.

### Photograph Three

Mrs. Standish thought that the woman in the photograph was part of a team of advertising executives. They were all solving a problem together and the woman had equal status with the men.

She described her work experiences using computer based technologies in the field of international banking. Mrs. Standish related how being a woman had affected her career in banking. "I think people have a tendency in the banking world to look at you and see that you are a woman initially, and make judgments right away. Men in particular and sometimes women, because women can discriminate against other women more harshly than men do at times." She stated that a women in banking will be allowed to go so far and no further. She described the negative treatment she received from her boss. He made demeaning comments to her in meetings and blamed her for situations that she was not responsible for. He also promised her a certain percentage of the growth of the business and then reneged on his promises. He gave her jewelry instead of money that was not the value of what she had contributed. Mrs. Standish thought that her boss believed he could get away with this behavior because she was a woman. She left the business world as a result of this experience.

### Photograph Four

Mrs. Standish looked at the women in the photograph and decided that she would like to be the woman in the yellow blouse because she looked very interested in the project she was working on. She said she also enjoyed working with people whereas the other woman seemed to be more of a secretary whose job was typing up documents.

Mrs. Standish recalled her experience at college learning about computers. She said that she was a little afraid at first and then realized that it was like learning another language. She purchased a computer and taught her husband basic computer skills. But since the computer was in his office, he's teaching her the things he has learned.

Mrs. Standish described diverse reactions to her use of computer based technologies. "Some people say, 'Oh, that's great,' and they also are computer users, and so they strike up a conversation. Other people say, 'Oh, gee, I never really use computers,' and some people say, 'I'm not even interested in using computers. I'm gonna get by without doing it.'"

### Photograph Five

Mrs. Standish looked at the women in the photograph and thought she was a working mother because of the way she was dressed. "She has office wear on and she's saying good-bye to her child." She thought the women in the photograph used the computer in the evenings and on weekends.

Mrs. Standish described her work responsibilities. She was teaching full time until she left to go on childcare leave. She used to share the household chores with her husband, but since her leave she does most of the housework. He sometimes gets the children ready for bed or helps with the dishes in the evening. Mrs. Standish and her husband are hoping to purchase a multimedia computer. She intends to use it when the children are napping. Mrs. Standish humorously suggested that her husband and she will fight over the use of the computer in the evenings. She has two children-the first child is two and a half and the second child is an infant.

## Photograph Six

Mrs. Standish suggested that the scene in the photograph might be a classroom where the young woman called over the teacher to ask her a question about something on the screen.

Mrs. Standish described three women she knows who use computer based technologies. She described her mother who had to start learning about computers at the age of fifty-three. She mentioned the draftsperson in her husband's office and a friend, who is also a neighbor.

Mrs. Standish indicated that her mother was the inspirational women in her life. She had stayed home when the children were growing up but she was very involved politically in community activities. After the children finished high school she began her career as a social worker. Mrs. Standish thought that her mother would have been "a real mover and shaker" if she had grown up in other times. She also mentioned her grandmother, who was ninety-five years old. She gave up her driver's license at the age of ninety. "She's very active in the garden club; she loves planting in her garden. She's interested in history; she's with the D.A.R. and she goes to all those meetings. Her mind is very alert, and yes, she's definitely inspired me a lot."

## Photograph Seven

Mrs. Standish reflected that the negative aspects of our computer culture were the fast pace of living and the rapid exchange of information.. However, she believed that computers were an incredible resource and tool for every aspect of our daily lives. She believed that computers have the potential for linking all schools in our country together. She predicted that teaching would be much more efficient because teachers can share lesson plans and do not have to "reinvent the wheel." She was hoping to return to the school she had worked in before her childcare leave, and set up a computer with a modem so that she could access NYCNET.

Mrs. Standish predicted a better life for girls in the future because they will have information at their fingertips. Children will be able to learn at their own pace. However, she predicted that regulation will be needed on the Internet to prevent children from viewing inappropriate material.

Mrs. Standish did not believe a computer would ever replace a teacher. She thought that girls and boys in the future will have equal computer skills. But she did not think that would affect gender equity. "I think equality for woman comes from us humans first. But computers will give women the power to move along in their careers just like men."

### Interview Three

Mrs. Standish suggested no corrections, one addition, and no deletions to the eight pages of narrative describing her experiences using computer based technologies:

*Addition one*—It was housed in a large closet.

She was shown the transcriptions from interviews' one and two used to develop the narrative. There were 30 pages from interview one and 41 pages from interview two.

After I gave a descriptive summary of feminist standpoint theory, I asked her for reactions and or experiences relating to the feminist perspective. Mrs. Standish stated that she was a feminist. She said that women need to be treated equally and given the choices that men have had all their lives. She also believed that women have to fight for these rights, opportunities, and choices.

Mrs. Standish described her introduction to feminism that was initiated by a male feminist professor. "He was an economics teacher, and he said that he was the biggest male chauvinist pig had I met him twenty years earlier when he lived in Europe. He was a businessman, and he didn't think women were important. Then he met his wife and she enlightened him. From that point on he has become a woman's advocate." Mrs. Standish indicated that this professor inspired her to be vocal about her feelings and thoughts with her family and friends. She believes feminism is most important (Transcript: Interview III, p. 8, 5/15/95).

## *Miss Garcia*

Miss Garcia is an undergraduate student in Education who is completing her B.A. in June. She is an Hispanic American, age 24, and single. Her parents are from Puerto Rico.

Miss Garcia was introduced to computers in the eighth grade. She describes a very positive initial learning experience:

I wasn't really nervous. I really was looking forward to working with it, because ever since computers started coming out, it was, like amazing: you wanted to see what computers could do. Once the teacher explained everything, you know, "This is what you are going to do," he gave us programs and you started working on the programs. It was basically simple programs so you started enjoying it. We had games so that was the best thing because we got a sense of how it was different from using it, your keyboard, instead of a joy stick. We all had partners, so we all enjoyed it.

And my teacher was my official teacher, so we knew more about computers, so we didn't even use textbooks. We did math programs and then we got the answer, which was simple. It's like in the computer you can think real quick, you know, you had the thinking right there, the brain right there.

When Miss Garcia went to high school she selected a pre-engineering course as an elective in her last year. In this drafting course, she used the computer to draw blueprints for her apartment. Her mother and father helped her to measure everything in the apartment and then the data were entered in the computer. She plans to continue using the computer for drafting, which she "loved," in the future.

At the present time, Miss Garcia has a computer at home which she uses to do wordprocessing in WordPerfect.

I am pretty much going into the detail part of it, reading the manuals and all. And I love it, because it's simple, it's fast, you know, I could type my work into it and I could see what I am doing, and I don't have to frustrate myself thinking of what if it's wrong or right or if I have to retype everything over again in order to fix it.

Miss Garcia obtained the computer she now has from her cooperating teacher during her student teaching experience:

She had one in the school, in the classroom, but it was stolen during the summer. The one that she sold me was her own personal computer. She had two of them so she had to get rid of the Commodore, the one that I have now. She has the IBM, so I was talking to her about getting a word processor, and she asked me if I was interested in buying a computer from her. So she gave me everything for $400 which was not bad. So I jumped immediately because I wanted a computer for a long time.

Interestingly, she shares this computer with all the members of her family, although she and her sister "chipped in together to pay for it." Her sister is studying science at Grant College. Her brother, who is majoring in music at another college, also uses this computer. Her ten year old sister, shares this computer time along with her oldest married brother who comes to visit and wants to work on the computer too. They all take turns. Miss Garcia is even trying to teach her mother, who wants to try it.

Miss Garcia is majoring in Bilingual education. Her desire to be a teacher was influenced by her first grade bilingual teacher. Whenever the teacher's assistant was absent, Miss Garcia was put in charge of half the group. She helped her classmates in reading and math. Her mother placed her in a bilingual kindergarten and first grade class; but her mother was afraid that she would come out speaking more Spanish than English:

> She put me in a regular English classroom after we transferred from one school to another. At first I understood her, but then when I got into the bilingual program, I understood that bilingual wasn't all of that, like teaching in one language and not learning the other. After I got into the program, I understood that bilingual is a program where you keep your native language, and appreciate where you're coming from, but you also get to learn another language, and you get to share these two languages with everyone else.

Miss Garcia visited Puerto Rico in 1985 and said she enjoyed the freedom of being able to go outside without parental permission.

> Here, even though the age I am, twenty-four, I still have to ask my mother if I could go out, or my father. I haven't been on a date for—I have not been on a date period. You could say that. My father's one that you have to have—whoever's picking you up, whoever your going out with, you have to be at home; that way he could know him. Now, he's that type, old- fashioned person. You know, because he makes it seem like this person's the one I'm going to marry, even though we're friends. So I said, "No, I am not going on a date." If I go to the movies I still have to ask my Mom if she needs me for something before I go to the movies, you know. My parents say the boys are treated the same way, but they're not. My sister and I see that they're not, because my sister is a year younger than me, and my brother who's eighteen years old—he gets more advantages to go out, to enjoy his life a little more, his social life a little more than we do. Yeah, we do see it. I see it especially, you

know, because my 27 year-old brother, when he was at home before he got married, he had a lot of advantages too. They're both treated differently than we are.

At the present time, Miss Garcia is taking two courses at Grant College. She is also working at her church on Saturdays as a volunteer teacher; she has been preparing sixteen students to receive the sacraments. Miss Garcia has been doing volunteer work for nine years.

Miss Garcia went to the computer lab in the college she attends but the experience she recalls was not pleasant:

> I only went once and I don't know, I was afraid, it was so confusing. It was a lot of programs and you have to wait for everyone else to finish whatever they're doing in order for you to print out the work. So, after once I went, I never went again. 'Cause it was like I hate waiting, first of all, I hate waiting for when I have to do a work and I'm in a rush to do it, and the computers are, I think, a little complicated for me. I prefer doing my own work on my own computer.

Miss Garcia's computer goals include learning more advanced programming and using the modem:

> I have the modem at home; the thing is I don't know how to use it. We need to get advanced into it. I have the Commodore, the Commodore's an old computer. Now you have the IBM and these advanced computers. The Commodore you hardly don't see anymore. Where could we get more programs for these old computers, the first computers that came out? I think there was Commodore and then came Apple, and the Apple is used a lot too, but the Commodore has something. I would like to get more information on that.

Miss Garcia forsees the ever growing presence of computer based technologies in the world of education:

> She will be growing in the modern world (little girl in photograph seven). This world will use a lot of technology, 'cause that's what we see, we're seeing a lot of technology in this planet. So by the time she becomes thirteen years old, maybe she'll have a computer teacher instead of a human being, you know, as a teacher. She will get to be more advanced than any other child would be in her age as she grows older.

## Responses to the Probes and Photographs

### Photograph One

Miss Garcia thought that both men and women were equally knowledgeable about computers.

She believed that she was knowledgeable in reading and math. She also enjoyed working with arts and crafts. Although she believed in women's intuition, Miss Garcia believed that it was her logical reasoning that helped to learn about computers.

### Photograph Two

Miss Garcia recalled her early learning experiences in science in elementary school. She remembered that the teachers were not enthusiastic about the subject. In fact, she thought the science lessons were more like reading lessons from a textbook.

Miss Garcia stated that she knew from first grade that she wanted to be a teacher. She was inspired by her first grade bilingual teacher who often put her in charge of a group of children when the assistant was absent. She remembered helping her friends in reading and math. However, Miss Garcia indicated that if she were given a second chance to choose a career it would be in the field of computer based technologies.

### Photograph Three

Miss Garcia looked at the woman in the photograph and thought she was a secretary.

Miss Garcia was not working but stated that being a woman has affected her personal life because she is always asked to teach the family whatever new things she has learned. Her mother depends on her a great deal and often volunteers her services to tutor the neighbor's children when they need help.

### Photograph Four

Miss Garcia looked at the two women in the photograph and thought that she would like to be the woman in the red blouse. Miss Garcia thought that the woman in red found her job interesting and she was independent because she worked alone whereas the woman in yellow seemed to need help.

Miss Garcia recalled her own initial learning experiences using a computer in the eighth grade. She remembered her computer teacher in junior high school because he made the class very interesting. She also remembered working with computers in high school when she enrolled in a pre-engineering drafting course.

Miss Garcia's family was very supportive about her computer learning. Her parents showed a great interest and her mother asked if Miss Garcia could teach her to use the computer.

Miss Garcia's responsibilities included helping her mother to clean the house and take care of the family. Although she was not working, she was enrolled in Grant College where she was taking courses to complete her degree. On Saturdays she volunteered to teach students preparing to take the Communion. She had sixteen students in her class at church.

## Photograph Five

Miss Garcia thought that if the woman in the photograph was not a working mother then she certainly should be. She believed it was the woman's responsibility to help her husband by going to work as well as taking care of the home and the family. "But I think a woman should prove to herself, no matter if she has children, she should also go to work and handle both being a mother and being a working mother."

## Photograph Six

Miss Garcia looked at the photograph and thought that this was a classroom in a college. The professor was explaining the computer program to the student. She thought that the professor was encouraging the female student to try to work through the program rather than the male. Miss Garcia believed that the personal attention given the female student would encourage her to continue learning about computers.

Miss Garcia said that she only knew two women who use computers and those women were her two sisters.

Miss Garcia described her mother as the most inspirational woman in her life. "She's always there for me, she always supports me, and she always given me the benefit of the doubt. I see her working at home seven days a week, day and night, and she's always there for us."

## Photograph Seven

Miss Garcia reflected on the photograph title "Improving with Age?" and agreed unconditionally that the changes resulting from computer based technologies were very good. She also thought that computers help us to understand that we can make changes and improve our world. She was unable to describe any negative impact of computer based technologies.

Miss Garcia predicted that the girl growing up in the modern world will encounter technology wherever she goes. She predicted that one day a computer will replace a human teacher. She believed that the child who will grow up under these conditions will be very advanced for her age. She will also have the choice of many career possibilities. Miss Garcia thought that many problems that we have today would disappear and girls growing up in the future would have a better chance for success.

### Interview Three

Miss Garcia offered *no* suggestions for addition, deletions, or corrections to the five pages of narrative describing her experiences using computer based technologies. She was shown the transcriptions from interviews' one and two used to develop the narrative. There were 19 pages from interview one and 24 pages from interview two.

After I gave a descriptive summary of feminist standpoint theory I asked her for reactions and or experiences relating to the feminist perspective. Miss Garcia stated that many people think that women are not equal to men but she believed that women work even harder than men because they have to take care of home responsibilities as well as job responsibilities. She also indicated that many people do not believe that women who work at home really work because they do not get paid. She believed that women who work at home have a full-time career.

Miss Garcia described the two points of view she held about the feminist perspective. She believed that women should be treated equally but she also understood the man's point of view who wanted a wife who could take care of household responsibilities as well as work. She considered herself neutral with regard to feminism. However, Miss Garcia was very concerned about the way the media portrayed women. "I think it's wrong, because it makes us, when we get disrespected, seem as if we are worthless—and we're not" (Transcript: Interview III, p. 6. 5/26/95).

# *Miss Escuto*

Miss Escuto is a special education teacher in a pre-school program. She has worked in this program for over two and a half years. She is an Hispanic American, age 27, and single. Her parents are from the Dominican Republic.

Miss Escuto's initial learning experience with computers occurred while she was a student in high school. Her class of freshman was chosen at random to start the introductory computer course in 1981:

> We were introduced to Basic language and we were one of the first schools that started introducing computers into the public education system. And it was very interesting and I learned to make programs. I was fourteen years old.

Miss Escuto's brother was also interested in computers and she had access to his computer at home. Then, something happened that resulted in her total avoidance of computers:

> My brother had a computer at home and I used to fidget with it, and I used to make programs, like I used to make a rocket ship that had my name on it and kept going like a countdown and would explode on the screen. And after that I don't know, I blanked out, because then, my brother was really interested into it, and all my cousins, and it became so technical that I just tuned out and forgot everything I learned, and I couldn't program it, a computer to turn on if I had to.

> It was so interesting, but then I guess as I got older it was boring and I just lost interest, total interest. And then I regretted it afterwards because it was—it just seemed so technical. And my brother was into—he had the whole set-up in his room with the modem, and he made friends in Texas and all over the place. He was good at it and he still is. I just thought it was boring, because to make the programs—I guess the computer languages were just coming up too fast, and by that time I just had one, then the next one would start, and it was just too much, and I was into other things, so I really didn't learn that.

Miss Escuto's brother continued his interest in computers and he now works with computers on his job.

He works with hazardous materials and they have computers in their vans sometimes, because if they're out of sight and they need some information that's in the main computer, and let's say if he's on duty and it's an emergency, two in the morning, they'll have the computer plugged in right there, and they can access any information from the main computer in the main building.

Interestingly, It was Miss Escuto's brother that revived her interest in computers again many years later.

He's sort of really like my link into computers because he's the one who told me he would get me a little laptop. Two years ago he brought it home and it was a tiny thing, it wasn't scary, and it was cute, and he showed me how to start it up and what I had to do and he was showing me: "If you have any questions, just press F-3 and it'll give you all the answers," and that's how I learned, trial and error.

Miss Escuto's laptop is programmed with MS-DOS, but her friends use Windows:

Now I'm getting interested and I know I have friends that have a Windows program, but now since I have a tiny lap-top that was just for my reports, now I wish I had a big computer and really get into Windows.

Miss Escuto uses her computer for her work with infants and pre-schoolers in a special education pre-school program in this city. It is a state funded school focusing on very young children with Downs Syndrome and seizure disorders. Pre-schoolers arrive for therapy sessions in the morning for two and a half hours. The infants arrive in the afternoon and stay until 3 o'clock. The children she is responsible for range in age from three weeks to five years of age. Miss Escuto's job involves parental training also.

It's interesting, but it's a lot of work and a lot of paperwork. I would guess more than other people, because on top of the lesson plans, you always have to keep on top of their I.E.P.'s where their goals are written for the year. And you know, yearly you have to write an evaluation where you discuss the child's social and emotional stage, and daily living skills-fine motor and gross motor.

It helps me in writing my evaluations, because they're time-consuming, and writing them out used to take me about two and a half hours and five to six pages, and then I had to wait ten days for the secretaries to type them at work. So I just had someone teach me the basic skills on how to access Word Perfect and type in and "save," and then someone else print it out for me on our machine , and that saved me at least two weeks of aggravation.

Miss Escuto did not have access to a computer at her school but the secretaries did. The director of her program, who is dyslexic, did not a have a computer.

He comes and goes, and he wants, you know, he works with the funding and with the Board of Directors, so he just basically has, you know, everybody do this, and it gets done. So when you're the boss, you get that kind of thing.

Miss Escuto is the first American citizen member of her family:

My whole family, my brother and everyone, I'm first American-born, so the whole computer technology is just way over their head for them (parents). My mother was from a small town. She has like a sixth grade education, and my father—I don't believe he finished high school. And my mother doesn't even speak English. My father speaks limited. He speaks English fairly well, I mean, he gets by, because he works in the street. He drives a truck, so he had to learn, but I don't think they ever came across a computer.

Miss Escuto learned to speak English in the public school system, however, Spanish is spoken exclusively in her home. She wants to be able to type in Spanish on her computer:

I really didn't start speaking English until I was in a day-care setting at—well, I was in day care early, eighteen months old, so I learned both languages simultaneously, but Spanish more because Spanish is spoken at home.

I would like to write things in Spanish on my computer, but then I would never be able to spell-check it. Since I am bilingual, I have a bilingual class in the mornings of pre-schoolers, and when I do the language section of their evaluation, you have to say the words that they're most common with, and a lot of times, if I write the word out in Spanish, I would really have to check to make sure it is correct. But it's bad because then it doesn't get the accent on it. But sometimes, depending on what mood I'm in, my last name has an accent on the "A," and you know, if I want to be fancy, I like to put the accent on the "A" and I can't do it on my computer, or the tilde on the end. On my reports for work, I had to write *niños*, children, and the second "n" is a "enya," with a tilde, and it has the tilde on the keyboard. But I couldn't get it to be on the top of the "n."

Miss Escuto has an avid desire to learn more about computers, and when she heard about a conference at one of the colleges, she was ready to sign up:

That's my next step, I want to learn more , and I just saw there was going to be a conference, but I asked, "Is it going to be more hands-on or lectures?" and they said "Lectures," and I said, "Oh, well, then no, 'cause I'm a hands-on learner." That's how I taught myself, was 'cause I had the computer right in front of me. If someone sat there and talked to me about it, I wouldn't assimilate it.

When my brother wasn't home I used to turn on his computer and work at it, and he used to tell me, "Here, read this book, and it'll tell you how to learn this." You know, how they have "DOS for Dummies" and all that. And I would say, "Okay, okay," and— when he'd leave and he'd go out in the evening, I'd just go and turn his computer on—and do whatever.

At the present time, Miss Escuto is majoring in elementary education. She is not majoring in Special Education, although she teaches in this area. Her bachelor's degree was in business, but then she changed careers. Her real desire is to work with immigrant children in a Bilingual Education program.

During the interview Miss Escuto's beeper went off and I asked her why she was wearing one.

Since I go to school one to two nights a week and my classes are usually three hours long and since I'm at least forty-five minutes from home, and also one night a week I volunteer at my church and I teach confirmation classes, and I belong to a fraternity from my church and we do a lot of things for the homeless, and we're trying to develop a AIDS respite home in my church, since I'm out a lot, I like my mother to keep track of me. You know, just my mother, my family, and my close friends have it as a way of keeping track of me. I would hate to be away and find out, something happened, since my Mom is home all day.

Miss Escuto concluded our session by relating the appeal she made to the youth of her church and their answer in the age of technology.

Just this Friday I had a lesson with the kids from my church and we were talking about materialism. And I think technology-wise, it is improving with age, I mean, what was available before to what is available now, and the prospects. The changes are great, but just like this picture is (photograph seven), it's like overshadowing the more basic parts, the more natural things that people take for granted. Just like sitting down and watching the sunset or helping someone or doing things for others—the basic things that technology can't do for you.

I was telling my kids, "You have to help, you have to serve, you have to help others and not expect things in return," you know—like we have the Spanish chorus's adults helping and full of people. And the English chorus where we have a younger population is only two or three girls singing every Sunday. "Well," I said, "What's going to happen when everyone that's doing things is gone now? And they answered,"Well, you know, we're recorded now, so just press 'play.'"

## Responses to the Probes and Photographs

### Photograph One

Miss Escuto said that from her experience she thought that men were more knowledgeable about computers than women. The women she knew enjoyed using the computer to do word-processing and to fix typing errors. However, the men she knew would talk for hours about computers.

Miss Escuto believed that her reasoning was more intuitive than logical. She thought that her intuition did not guide her to learn about computers until she had the need to know. But if she had been more logical she would have continued learning instead of waiting till she had to know about computers.

## Photograph Two

Miss Escuto remembered her early learning experiences in science. She recalled projects that involved charts and essays but she did not remember any type of manipulative materials or live animals.

Miss Escuto wanted to be a teacher when she was little. She was inspired by her second grade teacher who used to ask her to be the class monitor. This teacher would tell her through the years, "You should go into teaching, you should; you'd make a good teacher."

Miss Escuto said that if she had a second chance to choose a career she would have become a teacher from the beginning rather than studying business.

## Photograph Three

Miss Escuto looked at the woman in the photograph and though she might be someone who was teaching the men a new concept.

Miss Escuto thought that being a women has helped in her job working with infants which included a lot of diapering and toilet training that takes place in the classroom. She thought that she was selected for the position because people think a woman is compassionate and patient. Miss Escuto had one male assistant and one female assistant to help her with two classes—an infant class and a class of three and four year olds. However, people outside of school who are not familiar with her job think that she "mothers or babys" the children rather than that she teaches them. Miss Escuto said that her job required training and skill but people told her she just played all day.

## Photograph Four

Miss Escuto looked at the two women in the photograph and chose to be the woman in red who was working alone. She thought that the woman seemed to know what she was doing whereas the other woman had someone hovering over her and seemed less secure.

Miss Escuto recalled her early experiences working with computers. When she was a freshman in high school her class was randomly selected to learn about BASIC—a computer language. Then she stopped using computers for a long time but her need to write evaluations and reports revived her interest again. She indicated that her brother had a great influence on this interest because he and her cousins were always talking about computers. He gave her a laptop to renew her use of computers.

## Photograph Five

Miss Escuto thought the woman in the photograph was a working mother because she seemed to be greeting the baby on her arrival. She thought the man looked as if he had been home.

Miss Escuto described her responsibilities at work and at home. She indicated that she was responsible for planning the activities of her class. She was also in charge of the two assistants who helped her. She was responsible for developing short and long range goals for each child in her program. Miss Escuto trained the parents of these children in techniques to stimulate their physical motor development.

Miss Escuto was responsible for all the household chores in her apartment because she lived alone. However, her mother cooked for her each night. She said that she used her computer in the evening to type up reports and evaluations she needed for work. Miss Escuto attended classes at Grant College one night a week. She also volunteered to teach at her church one night a week. When she found time she also went to the gym in the evening.

## Photograph Six

Miss Escuto reflected on the scene in the photograph and thought it was a college classroom. She thought that the female student in the photograph was showing the male student something on the computer screen since she had her hand on the mouse.

Miss Escuto described three women she knew who used computers. She mentioned her co-worker who used the computer to type reports and evaluations. One of her friends at the church used the computer to make banners and invitation cards. She also described a third friend who used the computer on her job. She used Windows; Miss Escuto did not have Windows on her laptop.

Miss Escuto described her aunt, her father's sister, as the inspirational woman in her life. She said that her family is male oriented because there are thirty males and only five girls. Her grandmother had eight sons and one daughter. She said her aunt was a doctor, a gynecologist/obstetrician, in the Dominican Republic and the only professional in the family. She received a great deal of support from her brothers who were blue collar workers. She was not married and lived with her mother.

## Photograph Seven

Miss Escuto reflected on the photograph title "Improving with Age?" She indicated that she had recently discussed this subject with her students from the church. She thought that our society is too concerned with materialistic values and that technology is overshadowing our appreciation of nature and concern for human beings. She described one of her student's comments when she remarked that there were very few young people attending the English chorus and soon there may be none. The student replied that the services were on tape and whoever arrived at the church could just press "play."

Miss Escuto predicted that the little girl in the photograph would have many more opportunities available to her because there was a breakthrough for young women. She said that women in her classes are taking more initiative and being praised for it. She believed that women today do not have to go into traditional jobs but can be whatever they want to be. She cautioned that women need to be praised and supported because even if they are very capable they can be discouraged in our society.

## Interview Three

Miss Escuto suggested three corrections, one addition, and one deletion to the seven pages of narrative describing her experiences using computer based technologies:

*Correction one*—I have a lap-top that is just for my *reports.*

*Correction two*—The children she is responsible for range in age from three weeks to *five years* of age.

*Correction three*—Spanish *is* spoken exclusively at home.

*Addition one*—This is a church-related program.

*Deletion one*—*Saint* should be removed from the name of the church-related program.

She was shown the transcriptions from interviews one and two used to develop the narrative. There were 18 transcribed pages from interview one and 29 transcribed pages from interview two.

After I gave a descriptive summary of feminist standpoint theory, I asked her for reactions and or experiences relating to the feminist perspective. Miss Escuto stated that she had mixed reactions to the feminist perspective. She believed in feminism and women's rights but she was turned off by the media reports of radical feminists who "stomp all over and cause havoc." She believed that the media had influenced this negative attitude.

Miss Escuto described the differences she noted between men and women. She thought women were more versatile than men. She thought that men were "more one-track minded"—they wanted something and they went toward it—whereas women were less directional in their outlook. Mrs. Escuto related a critical incident that she experienced. A salesman called her at home and asked to speak to her husband. She explained that she did not have a husband and he became very flustered. He said that he wanted to speak to her husband about some information on data base and computer programming and the courses that are being offered. She said that he never even asked her if she was interested in taking these courses.

## *Mrs. Varsaw*

Mrs Varsaw is a substitute teacher, age 35, married and the mother of one young daughter (age 5). She is a recent immigrant from Europe. Mrs. Varsaw's initial computer experience began with a flyer she received in the mail from an institute. They offered financial aid to study computer technology, which would result in a secretarial position.

> This is experience, first experience with computer, wasn't very pleasure because the teacher was very strict and we learn all about how computer is built—technical information about computer. We were tested every two weeks, so it wasn't any pleasure. Most of us in the class were women, because we were prepared to work as secretaries. For men it was offered repair of refrigerators. Women in my class were from Russia, from Poland, and from China. We were tested in English, so I passed English and was put on third grade of this English and for the first semester I got also computer. Actually we didn't type on this computer, we just watched.

Mrs. Varsaw's second semester with computers was "horrible" since she was expected to type at least twenty-two words a minute with no mistakes and perfect margins.

> And at the end of the semester, there were a lot of younger women, especially black women, and they were doing very good, but for me, what was very difficult, to type twenty-two words. I was terrified, so I don't have a computer to practice, and typing at home

or a typewriter. In Europe, where I come from, everybody just
write handwrited, because type it wasn't so easy. The machines
were very expensive. I don't even say anything about a computer,
because at the beginning it was even nobody even dream about
computer. It was very very expensive in Europe.

Mrs. Varsaw was a teacher in Europe; she graduated from the
university and worked three years as an elementary school teacher.
She was granted a professional diploma.

Pay in Europe was terrible. For example, if computer cost here two
thousand dollars, it's a lot of money, but if you earn even three
hundred dollars per week, you can save for this. In Europe was
impossible. I earn ten thousand zloty—it was like twenty, thirty
dollars a month. But—what was maybe good about Europe: They
pay for our apartment and they pay for our ride to school. We got
eighteen hours per week. So it was nothing. You couldn't survive
with those kind of money. But it was a wonderful experience; the
discipline was very good; the children were nice.

We don't have any technology. If I want to give some tests I'm
supposed to write for everybody. Maybe now—I'm here already
five years and I spend more than year in a refugee camp in Austria.

Mrs Varsaw left the institute after the second semester when she
learned from a Russian student in the class that it was possible to enroll
in Grant College and continue her teaching career in America.

But I came here, I took four trains, and I couldn't believe it. I spent
almost two hours to get here. And when I get to Sandman Avenue,
I didn't see the school, and I wanted to go back, you know, and go
back to take train and go home. But I was thinking and "I try to go
somewhere, maybe—a— a—" And I saw this Grant College. And
that was the first step.

While attending Grant College, Mrs.Varsaw enrolled in E.S.L.
courses. The tutoring center for remedial help was housed in a computer
lab.

I wanted to write properly, and so I took writing course and reading
course. My professor told me, "Just go to tutoring center and take
one tutor and work between courses." We met only twice a week

and it's not enough to learn English. So I went to tutoring center and I worked with one girl there. We were typing on the computer. They've got IBM there. She taught me step by step how to use this, and again we were typing my essays, so we were typing. She told me how to do this.

Mrs. Varsaw decided to buy a computer as a result of an incident that occurred while she was taking a sociology course for her masters' degree.

I've got sociology last semester, and the professor was very hard. We were supposed to write every two weeks one paper, about every philosopher like Marx or Engels. So, she wanted to write every detail about his life. So I went to the library for the first time to find some information there about Marx. They've got many encyclopedias, and I was looking, and it was pages and pages. I really didn't know what to do.

So I got a neighbor and they've got a ten-year old. Last summer they bought him a computer. I went to him and asked him, "Do you got some information? I really need this information, but specific information, not like a Britannica, they got many pages, and I don't know what information is important or not." I went to him and I was amazed how he was working at this computer. And I asked him, "How do you know everything? He is in P.S. 539 in this city. He is taking computer courses. It was amazing for me. Yes, and he found me and print me some good information. And his father asked me , "Do you like this, though?" "I love this." "So buy one." I've got a lot of expenses right now, but I promised myself that I buy; when I graduate here, the next year I buy a computer.

Mrs. Varsaw spoke to her husband about her decision, and he agreed, but her problem is time.

And I told even my husband that I have to buy the computer, so he told me, "So buy." But money is not the problem, you have to have time to work with the computer. Right now I sub for a Catholic School. And I got four courses. I take 702, that is the Master's thesis and Perspective on the Holocaust. I took Puerto Rican Community, and political science.

Interestingly, Mrs. Varsaw considers the course, *Perspective on the Holocaust*, her own personal holocaust experience.

Everybody understand that holocaust is terrible thing that happened in Europe. Because the concentration camps were built in Europe. The German built concentration camps and the European people had to help them. There is no other way to survive. Most of the Jews actually were killed in Europe because these camps were the biggest factory of death. And the professor was also a survivor. That even is even worse for me. The professor can't say something like this, "I hate Europeans," but students can say whatever they want. They are very angry. Many Jews were killed. "Why they didn't help?" I really don't know much about holocaust, because my city was always under German influence. It was a free city and the Germans settled there. Actually I took this course because Professor Block told me, "Oh take this course. You know, she is also a Jew.

(Note: Professor Block is not Jewish, but of German extraction. But ironically Professor Block might have thought that Mrs. Varsaw was a Jewish refugee from Europe, but in fact she is Catholic.)

Mrs. Varsaw is also interested in buying a computer for her five year old daughter:

I also need this computer for my daughter. She doesn't have any experience yet, but I don't know, buy some programs for her because I heard from my friend that there are programs for math, and for reading, even some tests, so they can learn how to read. So it's very interesting.

Mrs. Varsaw has only been in America for five years. When she left Europe she could not speak a word of English or German; she spoke the language of her country and Russian. "But I've always been very ambitious. In Austria, actually they speak German, and in one year I spoke German." Mrs. Varsaw left Europe with her brother and her best friend. It wasn't easy; she describes the ruse she played on her principal:

So I lied to my Principal that we get to Greece, because in Greece wasn't a refugee camp. So because if somebody tells, "We are going to Austria" or "We are going to Germany," that's mean you are going to a refugee camp. I told the Principal, "We are only leaving for one week, and we will be there for only one week." So I think, he wouldn't believe it that we leave, because I wasn't so strong. I was not mentally strong like my friend. She was a very strong person. I felt like something who couldn't survive with no help with my brother. Now I feel strong, much better about my abilities. I got these strong feelings about myself from this holocaust experience at Grant College. But you know you have to have some horrible experience—even I've got "C," because they obviously hate me, but what can I do? I've got most of my grades I've got "A," so even if I get a "C," I can survive. Most of the professors were very good. You couldn't believe what kind of professor we've got in Europe in university: They are like gods, and you are nobody.

Women are treated worse than men in Europe. They are not smart, they can't do some stuff you know. They've got home women, stay at home and take care of children, and men are going out and even take some other women, but the wives are supposed to sit at home and take care of children and men are doing whatever they want. And they don't share they activities at home, for example, laundry and cooking and everything. It's like women supposed to do this. I feel better in America, but I didn't train my husband, my husband is still European and thinks like this.

Mrs. Varsaw described the changes in technology in Europe since she has left.

But now, 1995, now is different, because we don't have Communism any more and many Western companies and everybody are moving to Europe. My parents and my two brothers are living there still. My youngest brother is in computer school right now. It's two years after high school. He took two years of computer school. But he wrote me a letter that he is very disappointed about the school because it's very difficult. Of course it's difficult, because you are supposed to type on the computer, you are supposed to know everything, you are supposed to know programs on the computer. They are tested all the time. It's very difficult , a lot of stress.

And my best friend, actually she is working with the computer for a company in Austria, in Vienna. Because she couldn't get a visa to the United States and to Canada. Because at this time they get visas only to Canada to only very skilled people, like my brother. He is a electronic engineer. He was excellent student in polytechnic in Europe, so they took him to Canada.

I was his sister, so—actually I was for them I was nobody: "Oh, a teacher? Who is teacher?" You know, from Europe, with no English. So they took me to Canada, because I was his sister. Because they don't separate families. They've got this policy. It wasn't difficult to get to the United States, and my husband wanted to get to the

United States because they are from another part of Europe, and almost everybody has this dream about the United States. I am from my city, almost half the population is in Germany, so we've got a different story. But he wanted to get badly to the United States. So I get too.

## Responses to the Probes and Photographs

### Photograph One

Mrs. Varsaw stated that women were better at typing and using simple programs but when people speak of successful computer programmers, they speak of men. Women are in offices working on word-processing programs that are very simple. She described a neighbor's son who made a great deal of money after he had taken a one year computer course. He had learned seven programs that year. Mrs. Varsaw reasoned that women were much busier than men who had more time to spend learning about computers.

Mrs. Varsaw believed that there were two types of women. Successful women were equal to men in ability and could do anything. Regular women, however, were just concerned with the care of the family.

Mrs. Varsaw believed that she thought logically rather than intuitively and that logical reasoning helped her to learn about computers.

### Photograph Two

Mrs. Varsaw recalled her learning experiences in elementary school in Europe. She said that she did not have a science teacher that did experiments. She was in a very small village school and one teacher taught all subjects. The classes were very small. Mrs. Varsaw said that she always wanted to be a teacher; she took care of her younger brothers and therefore grew up as a teacher.

Mrs. Varsaw said that she made an independent choice to study computers. She reflected that most immigrants go to work to earn money and support the family. She thought that if she had not met her Russian friend in the institute who told her about Grant College she would probably be working with computers today.

### Photograph Three

Mrs. Varsaw thought that the woman in the photograph was a very smart and intelligent woman who was working on the same level as the men in the photograph. She thought they were probably solving some difficult problem with the computer program they were running.

Mrs. Varsaw said that being a woman did not affect her career as a teacher because most teachers were women. She thought that women don't have to compete with men in these jobs, but if they work with computers, "The first position goes to the men and only lower positions go to women."

## *Photograph Four*

Mrs. Varsaw looked at the two women in the photograph and decided that she would like to be the woman in the yellow blouse. This woman reminded her of the successful and intelligent woman in photograph three who was also wearing a yellow blouse. She thought that the other woman in red looked like a student who was typing up something.

Mrs. Varsaw explained that she enrolled at the institute to learn about computers because it was easier to find a job in America if you have computer skills. Her teaching license from Europe was not valid in America. She had hoped that after completing the course at the institute she would be able to find a better job than cleaning apartments for people.

She decided to purchase a computer when she realized that the computer could access information that she needed for school. Her neighbor's young boy sparked her interest in computers. Her husband was very agreeable and supportive about her desire to purchase a computer because he thought that everybody should know about computers today. He also thought it would help their younger child with her school work.

## *Photograph Five*

Mrs. Varsaw thought that the woman in the photograph was not a working mother because she had a baby to take care of. She said that the woman was wearing clothes that would be worn at home rather than on the job.

Mrs. Varsaw described her responsibilities at home and at work. She indicated that she does the cooking, cleaning, laundry and shopping for the family. Her husband sometimes helps her with the shopping.

Mrs. Varsaw said that she would love to learn more about computer programs but she does not have the time. She thought that after she completed her master's degree she would have more free time. She wanted to find a job as a teacher in the public school system. After school in the evenings she promised herself that she would study more about computer programs.

## Photograph Six

Mrs. Varsaw thought that the scene in the photograph was a classroom. She described the young woman as a student who was learning a computer program. The older woman was a teacher who is helping her with a problem. Mrs. Varsaw thought that the older woman was angry about something but then she thought that the older woman was explaining the use of the mouse.

Mrs. Varsaw described three women who use computers. She mentioned a neighbor who worked in an office with computers. This woman was always telling her about the difficulties she was having learning new programs required by her company. Mrs. Varsaw remembered her neighbor downstairs who used a computer and an American woman who had learned about computers from the time she was a child in school.

Mrs. Varsaw described her mother as the inspirational women in her life. She was not educated but she encouraged Mrs. Varsaw to finish school and graduate in Europe. Mrs. Varsaw said she went through very tough times in the school because the teachers were very strict and they screamed all the time. If it were not for her mother, Mrs. Varsaw believed she would never have gone back to school after an incident that occurred.

## Photograph Seven

Mrs. Varsaw looked at the photograph title, "Improving With Age?" She agreed that everything is improving all the time in our society. She reflected that it was difficult to learn new things because she did not have the time needed for learning. She said that computer technology was changing so fast that she did not have the time to learn the new programs or how to use the more complicated computers.

Mrs. Varsaw believed that computers should never replace teachers but that computers in the classrooms can inspire children to choose a career in computers. She recalled that there were many computers in the parochial school she substituted in but there were no trained teachers to use them. "Probably—in parochial school, and I think they bought the computers but nobody use these computers, so I observe for two months."

Mrs. Varsaw believed that children were spending too much time playing games on the computer. She thought that they were becoming addicted to the computer.

Mrs. Varsaw predicted that life will become very difficult for women in the future who do not have computer skills. She thought that the competition to find jobs will be terrible and only those women who have computer skills will survive. She thought that there will always be a need for teachers in the future because they not only teach students how to behave but they also teach them about their beliefs and values which a computer cannot do.

She predicted that women who are very capable will be able to compete with men but that "regular women" who have children and get married will never be equal to men.

## Interview Three

Mrs. Varsaw suggested one correction, one addition, and no deletions to the seven pages of narrative describing her experiences using computer based technologies:

*Correction one*—Public School Number.

*Addition one*—And at the end of the semester, there were a lot of women, *especially black women.*

She was shown the transcriptions from interviews' one and two used to develop the narrative. There were 52 transcribed pages from interview one and 38 transcribed pages for interview two. The total of ninety pages was the highest of all the respondents. As Mrs. Varsaw read her narrative she said, "I didn't think my life was so important. It's like a story in a book."

After I gave a descriptive summary of feminist standpoint theory I asked her for reactions and or experiences relating to the feminist perspective. Mrs. Varsaw thought that feminism was a great movement in America. She recalled that women are not paid the same as men for the same work they do; but women in America can fight for a higher position in society.

Mrs. Varsaw indicated that she considered herself a feminist here in America but it would have been impossible in the country that she came from because women in her country need someone to help them financially, therefore "men are basic for every women in Europe." Mrs. Varsaw thought that women in America can survive on their own; they were very fortunate to be born in this country and have a career (Transcript: Interview III, p. 5, 5/23/95).

*Chapter V*

# A Case and Cross-Case
# Thematic Analysis

This chapter presents an in-depth analysis of the narratives of the nine professional women in education who use computer based technologies. The first section consists of a thematic analysis of each of the cases. The multiple themes derived from each of the cases was arrived at through a process that began with the coding of the data. After a time of reflection and incubation, this researcher developed a matrix of categories derived from the research questions. When the evidence from the data for each case was arrayed across the six categories, multiple themes emerged. The second section of this chapter consists of a cross-case analysis of the data. After examining the themes derived from each of the cases, these themes were compared and revised to consider new patterns. Details of each case were compared until pattern matching of the themes revealed new understandings and a search for explanation-building. This was a process that was repeated many times (Yin, 1989, p. 115). Section three of this chapter attempts to use Feminist Standpoint Theory as a basis for analysis in order to shed new light on the narratives..

The discovery of cultural themes, however, cannot precede without defining what themes are. Ely (1991) defines a theme, as follows:

A theme can be defined as a statement of meaning that 1) runs through all or most of the pertinent data, or 2) one in the minority that carries heavy emotional or factual impact. It can be thought of as the researcher's inferred statement that highlights explicit of implied attitudes toward life, behavior, or understandings of a person, persons, or culture. (p. 150)

Spradley's definition (1980) of a cultural theme adds further clarification to this concept:

For purposes of ethnographic research I will define a cultural theme as any principle recurrent in a number of domains, tacit or explicit, and serving as a relationship among subsystems of cultural meaning. A cognitive principle is something that people believe and accept as true and valid; it is an assumption about the nature of the commonly held experience. Themes are assertions that have a high degree of generality. (p. 141)

Themes in qualitative research are grounded in the data and are usually written as assertions in which the researcher attempts to understand the point of view of the participant. This process is a creative act that demands total immersion in the data. Categories are listed and refined as one attempts to search for similarities and contrasts among them. Themes may include the actual words of the participants or they may be "distilled from the data in as close a likeness as possible of the participant's mode of expression" (Ely, 1991, p. 154). The themes derived from an inductive analysis of each case in this study were used to compare findings for commonalties or patterns across cases.

The second section of this interpretive process, the cross-case analysis, highlights the patterns evident in the themes. Differences are noted and explained in the context of the life histories of these women of the computer generations. The researcher's objective in this strategy is to generate new insights relating to these nine professional women in education and their use of computer based technologies.

Section three of this analysis attempts to use Feminist standpoint theory as a basis for pattern-matching. Yin (1989) defines pattern-matching as one of the most desirable strategies for case-study analysis: "Such a logic compares an empirically based pattern with a predicted one. If the patterns coincide, the results can help a case study to strengthen its *internal validity*" (p. 109). This last section of the analysis will answer the third research question in this study: To what extent does the feminist perspective shed light on the personal narratives of these professional women in education relative to their use of and experience with computer based technologies?

# Thematic Analysis of the Cases

## Case One: Professor O'Grady

Professor O'Grady's remembrance of her childhood days revealed the little girl whose future dream was to become a teacher. Although Professor O'Grady's mother believed a woman's place was in the home, she had inspirational teachers who motivated her to develop "intellectual life." Her memories include doing "natural stuff"—science experientially learned outside of school. In high school, however, the nuns who were her teachers not only taught science but also encouraged her educational pursuits. Poverty and sickness in her family limited her choices after high school; she had to work in an insurance company because of the family's financial problems.. She soon realized that she was not a "policy form person" and the need for emotional connections compelled her to leave the insurance job and go into teaching.

As a college professor she encountered discrimination in the workplace because she was a woman. She was also sensitive to inequities in the workplace between the haves and the have-nots. For example the differential use that educators make of computer technology, depending on the social class of children. She wished that one day she could go back to elementary school teaching and reverse the gender stereotypes of girls who were "scared of frogs and things." She also expressed disappointment at the lack of professional support that she received from other women faculty members. Her colleagues' avoidance of conversations about computers also prevented any opportunity for computer networking in the workplace.

She described the frustration she experienced at the department's refusal to provide a computer for her office. However, she did have access to many male links to computer learning in the faculty computer lab and in computer courses offered at the college. Interestingly, she believed that logical reasoning and her ability to figure things out through experiential learning were the key factors that aided her computer learning. She talked about the incredible technological changes she has seen since her first computer experience on a mainframe and emphasized the importance of the time factor in learning about telecommunications. She thought that teachers needed time to learn telecommunications if they are to prepare to teach the next generation. Professor O'Grady also described the need for emotional connections that must exist between a teacher and student. She revealed the strong emotional connections and concern that she had for her own children who were sophisticated users of computer based technologies.

Professor O'Grady described the daily chores of women's work that was not shared in the family. She hoped that computer based technologies would one day enable women to work at home and free up both husband and wife.

Professor O'Grady recognized the importance of the feminist perspective in providing women opportunities for choices that she never had. But she resented feminists who were women with a viewpoint that would not accept her choice of a career and many children. These dual perspectives were also evident as she described her daughter's experience of discrimination in the workplace. She stated that she was not a feminist but underscored the fact that women are not valued intellectually for themselves but are seen first as good looking women and then, "What else can you do?"

## *Case Two: Mrs. Intel*

Mrs. Intel's remembrance of childhood days revealed the little girl whose future dream was to become a scientist, although she did not know any scientists nor did she remember anything about science in elementary school. Her perceptions of woman's capabilities may be inferred from her choice of inspirational teachers as her role models rather than her mother who loved her but did not inspire her. "She was too passive." Her seventh grade math teacher encouraged her to love math through experiential learning. Mrs. Intel stated that he was the one who gave her the confidence to later learn about computers. After high school she planned to study architecture; but family problems intervened and limited her choices. Her boyfriend, who was studying about computers, became her male link to computer learning. She was so intrigued with his work on the mainframe that she went on to study computer programming. This job was necessary to help with the financial needs of her family.

As a computer programmer she experienced discrimination in the workplace because she was a woman. She was denied opportunities for promotion and told a woman's place is in the home taking care of the children. She also described discriminatory practices in the workplace relating to racial prejudice. Her need for emotional connections eventually led her into education where "people were concerned about people rather than stocks and bonds."

As an intern in education Mrs. Intel used the computer to do statistical studies of children's mathematical skills in her elementary school class. At the same time she worked part time as an assistant manager in the college science lab. This provided her with the opportunity to introduce her four high school interns to computers. She remarked on the differences between the boys who enjoyed playing games on the computer and the girl who did not feel comfortable having fun.

Mrs. Intel described the partnership she had with her husband who shared the woman's work of raising the children and running the home. She was also a PTA volunteer when her children were younger. She remembered the computers on display in the public school and never used because of the need for trained teachers. Her son, however, became a computer teacher because of her influence; an example of women sharing computer knowledge with men.

Mrs. Intel also recalled inspiring other women to learn about computers when her company was computerizing clerical jobs. She was also computer networking with her former boss and the women she met in the science lab.

Mrs. Intel described the need for emotional connections in students' learning experiences. She did not believe it was healthy for children to sit in front of a computer screen without moving their bodies or talking to other youngsters. She explained that computers were wonderful tools but they were not a substitute for teachers. Her predictions for the future revealed that girls would encounter computers in the workplace of the future because they would be part of whatever she does.

Mrs. Intel stated that she was a feminist just as she was an anti-racist or against bigotry when she found discrimination in the workplace. She recognized that there were many different women with this viewpoint—feminists who were also egomaniacs and show-offs. However, she thought feminism was necessary and good.

## Case Three:  Miss Bell

Miss Bell's remembrance of childhood revealed the little girl whose future dream from the age of eight was to become a teacher.   She recalled how fortunate she was to have science teachers who used experiential learning methods.   Her stepmother and her teachers were the inspirational women in her life.

Miss Bell was appointed principal as a result of affirmative action legislation that prevented discrimination against women and other minorities.   However, she stated that once on the job women have to prove themselves more than men.   She experienced discrimination in the workplace; the men did not take her seriously and the women challenged her authority.   As a principal she became aware of the many opportunities for computer use in the schools:  attendance and information gathering, grant writing, and word-processing.   She recognized the importance of telecommunications to access the Internet and search the databases for her students.   She considered the computer a great time-saver.   She was also aware of the disparity between the obsolete Commodores her students used in their computer lab and the state of the art equipment in more affluent schools.   She worked with her PTA to change this disadvantage between the haves and the have-nots.   Miss Bell accessed computers as part of a job in college but it was not until she became a principal that she was motivated to buy a state of the art home computer.   Although her male links to computer learning were her assistant principal and computer teacher, she stated that when she was learning a program on her own, she used intuition and experiential learning.   Miss Bell used her computer an hour or two a day but she realized that computer learning required time and it was the time factor that prevented her from exploring telecommunications.

Women's work for Miss Bell included the care of a two-family home as well as a full time job as principal and a part time job as college instructor.   During her free evenings she encouraged her friend Juan to surf the Internet on her home computer; an example of women sharing computer knowledge with men.

Miss Bell had known many women who use computers.   She networked with her aunt who was a college professor and her cousin who was a computer analyst.   Her two sisters were also part of this computer network.

Miss Bell believed that computer based technologies of the future will produce many incredible technological changes including communication with someone on another planet.   She predicted many more choices and opportunities for girls that will reverse gender stereotypes. She warned, however, of the isolation and lack of socialization of many students who used computers. She emphasized the need for emotional connections and communication links for students of today and tomorrow.

Miss Bell did not consider herself a feminist. She recognized that men and women have different perceptions but she believed that it was important to emphasize our emotional connections rather than our differences if we are to live together as an educational community.

## *Case Four: Dr. Goldman*

Dr. Goldman's remembrance of childhood days revealed the little girl whose future dream was to become a wanderer and travel around the world. She attended the yeshiva, where she learned to love poetry and language. Dr. Goldman's mother who was also her English teacher was the inspirational woman in her life.

Women's work for Dr. Goldman consisted of a full time teaching position in the elementary school. After school she directed the puppet center at Grant College, taught courses, and shopped and cooked for the family. Her interest in the computer awakened when she realized she could use desk top publishing to tell stories. She indicated that she was not interested in the technical aspects of how the computer works. But her need for emotional connections motivated her to access the Internet and communicate with other people on-line. She also used telecommunication to find grants and funding for her center. Interestingly, she stated that she did not discuss her use of computer based technologies with colleagues or friends. Therefore computer networking was none existent.

Dr. Goldman's opportunity to learn about computers began in an adult education course; where because of poor attendance, she learned how to turn a computer on and off. Her computer skills were learned experientially at home with a friend. Afterwards she hired a tutor, who was a computer major, to help her apply graphics to the resource manual she was writing. Interestingly, this was her second male link to computer learning; her son also used the computer substantially in his work. The need for emotional connections resulted in giving her computer a name. "I'm getting to know my computer personally. I call it Wilbur. It's like a child or spouse. It's someone to talk to. It's company."

Dr. Goldman believed that the effect of computer based technologies will be to create a society in which there are stratified classes based on the criteria of computer literacy. Girls who do not have computer skills will lead a difficult life, however, girls who are computer literate will reverse gender stereotypes because of unlimited future possibilities and work options. She predicted that the next generation will begin to learn about computers in kindergarten. However, Dr. Goldman believed that the need for emotional connections was the reason the computer would never replace teachers because computers have no emotion.

Dr. Goldman shared her dual perspectives on the subject of feminism. She appreciated the choices that were now possible for women but she wanted the perks that go with being a woman. She stated that she was not a radical feminist. She reflected on the discrimination that is still apparent in the workplace when men are promoted over women who could do the job better. Her perceptions of woman's capabilities were evident in her descriptions of women in authority. She believed that woman in authority can use their feminine personality and ability to create a work force where employees were motivated, enthusiastic, and the morale was high.

## Case Five:  Mrs. Varsaw

Mrs. Varsaw's remembrance of childhood days revealed the little girl whose future dream was to become a teacher. She attended school in a village in Europe where the teachers were strict and highly respected. Her mother was the inspirational woman in her life who although she was not educated, encouraged her daughter to finish school and graduate. Mrs. Varsaw became a teacher in Europe. She experienced discrimination in her flight from Europe to Canada with her brother. Although she was a teacher she did not meet the criteria for acceptance; she gained entry to Canada on the basis of her brother's qualifications as an electrical engineer.

Women's work for Mrs. Varsaw consisted of substitute teaching at a parochial school during the day, taking courses at the college in the evening, and cooking, cleaning, and shopping in her spare time. It was at this parochial school that she recognized the need for trained computer teachers.

Mrs. Varsaw's opportunity to learn about computers began when she enrolled in a computer course at the Institute in order to obtain a job in America. She was aware of differences in the computer culture between women who type and use simple computer programs and men who were successful computer programmers. She also noted that there was a time factor that encouraged these differences. Women were much busier than men who had more time to spend learning about computers. She expressed the desire to learn more about computers but could not find the time. She recognized that the incredible technological changes taking place in computer software programs required time for learning.

Mrs. Varsaw's male links to computer learning were her neighbor's young son who helped her with information for a college course using his computer and her younger brother who was enrolled in a computer school in Europe. She stated that since her departure great technological changes had taken place in Europe.

Mrs. Varsaw had many friends and neighbors with whom she shared stories about the effects of computers in the workplace but she did not engage in any technical discussions relating to computer networking.

Mrs. Varsaw believed that computers in the schools can inspire students by providing new choices for career opportunities in the field of computers. She worried that children who played with computer games may become addicted and isolated. She stressed the need for human teachers and emotional connections that socialized children in traditional beliefs and values. She also warned about a future society of haves and have-nots where competition for jobs will be terrible for girls who do not have computer skills.

Mrs. Varsaw believed that feminism was a great movement in America that reversed gender stereotypes. She recalled the discrimination against women in her country where women were not considered smart. In Europe the women's place was in the home caring for the children, cleaning and cooking while the men went out to do whatever they wanted.

## *Case Six: Miss Lee*

Miss Lee's remembrance of childhood days revealed the little girl whose future dream was to become a gold medalist in roller skating and a teacher. Her mother, who worked in a factory as a seamstress to support the family, was the inspirational woman in her life. She also recalled her first grade teacher whose kindness and care of the children inspired her to want to become a teacher. Although Miss Lee began her college studies as a business major the need for emotional connections influenced her decision to change careers and go into teaching.

Woman's work for Miss Lee included a full time job as a kindergarten teacher during the day, a part time job teaching workshops in the Grant College science lab after school, and coursework for her Masters degree in the evening. She was also responsible for preparing the evening meal for the family.

She contrasted her science classes in elementary school where she listened and learned from textbooks with the workshops she has given in science that emphasized experiential learning. She noted that there are differences between girls and boys because of cultural stereotyping. These differences, she reflected, were the reason women were more familiar with life experiences rather than technical things like computers. She expressed frustration at the discrimination she experienced in the workplace resulting from her age rather than her sex. She thought young woman teachers were not appreciated and not expected to know too much. Miss Lee wanted to have a computer in her classroom. Some of her children played computer games at home while others did not know what a typewriter was. She wanted to reverse this inequity between the haves and the have-nots.

Miss Lee's opportunity to learn about computers began in sixth grade where she learned how to scroll her name across the screen. Later, however, as a business major she learned computer skills. She expressed regret that she did not learn to access the Internet but lack of time prevented her. She wanted more time to explore the Internet through experiential methods. She believed that her intuition helped her to explore unfamiliar computer software programs.

Miss Lee's male link to computer learning was her uncle who was a computer programmer. She also had friends who used computers but Miss Lee did not engage in computer networking because as she indicated, "I'm not one to talk about it."

Miss Lee predicted incredible technological changes in the future that would result in women working at home on computers that were smaller than a briefcase while doing the family thing. She wondered as an educator if the best method to teach the computer was experientially through play—the way she had learned about computers—by getting ideas and trying them out. Miss Lee did not believe that computers would ever replace a teacher because of the need for emotional connections. "Computers can't give you emotional support, only humans can."

Miss Lee expressed dual perspectives in her thoughts about feminism. She believed that women should encourage each other to stand up for their rights but while she had feminist ideals she was not politically involved. She described feminists who were women with a viewpoint. "Some feminists are hypocritical because they want certain rights that men want yet they want standards lowered." She believed that there were some things that women could not do because of physical differences or because society restrained them. But she wanted women to be treated as women.

## Case Seven: Mrs. Standish

Mrs. Standish's remembrance of childhood days revealed the little girl whose future dream was to become a baton twirler, and then a teacher, and later a scientist. She remembered that even then there were differences between her brothers' interests and her interests. She enjoyed playing with dolls or playing house while her brothers played with Legos and GI Joes. Her mother and grandmother were the inspirational women in her life. In school she had math teachers who gave her confidence in math through experiential learning methods. Her father was a professional athlete which was reflected in the mobility of the family during her early years. She had many choices during those years. She actively participated in field hockey, lacrosse, and dancing and swimming competitively. But after her parent's divorce she had to work to support herself through school.

Mrs. Standish began her career in investment banking. But because of the discrimination she experienced in the workplace, she left business to go into teaching. She believed that now there were changes in gender stereotyping in schools which resulted in girls having access to computers at an early age. Mrs. Standish believed that this access will permit girls to succeed in computer based technologies as well as mathematics and science. She also noted the disparity in her school between children who were computer literate and those who were not. Her future dream was to go back to teaching and bring Logo back to her school. She believed that this computer program in math would close the gap between the haves and the have-nots.

Mrs. Standish's opportunity to learn about computers began in sixth or seventh grade. The computer that the class used was very large and had a modem. There was a large time gap between that experience and her next experience using a computer as an international business major in college. Her male links to computer learning began in the college computer lab. She asked the students some questions to get her started and continued to learn by experimenting. She used this same experiential learning method of figuring things out in the Logo computer course she took at Grant College. The professor gave her very few instructions.

Mrs. Standish purchased a computer for use at home but after teaching her husband how to use it he "stole" the computer when he moved his office from the home. She cannot afford to buy another computer now because of financial considerations. However, she uses Microsoft Excel for Windows when she goes to her husband's office to help him with his business. Interestingly, her husband was now her male link to computer learning as he taught her things he had learned. She was very excited about her children growing up in the next generation where the CD-ROM and multimedia have unlimited possibilities.

Women's work for Mrs. Standish included the care of two infants as well as the cleaning, cooking, and other household chores. Since she was on childcare leave from school she had enrolled in courses at Grant College to complete her Masters degree. Interestingly, when she was teaching, her husband shared in the household chores. Since she has been on childcare leave, she does most of the housework.

Mrs. Standish has many women friends and acquaintances who use computers. She networks with them about the incredible technological changes in our society resulting from computer based technologies but does not discuss technical aspects of computer use.

Mrs. Standish believed that computers are an incredible resource for teachers that will one day link schools together. She acknowledged that teachers were afraid that computers would one day replace them but she did not consider this a possibility. She believed that children's need for emotional connections would prevent a computer from ever replacing a teacher. She predicted that computers will help children to learn more at a younger age, but the next generation will also learn at their own pace. She expressed the need to regulate computer programs so that youngsters who accessed the Internet would be limited in their choices to programs that do not contain objectionable material for children.

Mrs. Standish described herself as a feminist because she believed that women needed to be treated equally and given the opportunities and choices that men have had all their lives. Her economics professor at college was a woman's advocate and a feminist. She considered him one of her most inspirational teachers. Mrs. Standish also believed that this present research involving women subjects would help in reversing many years of gender stereotyping.

## *Case Eight: Miss Escuto*

Miss Escuto's remembrance of childhood days revealed the little girl whose future dream was to become a teacher. Her second grade teacher was her inspiration; this teacher encouraged her to go into teaching. Miss Escuto chose her aunt who was a doctor in the Dominican Republic as the inspirational woman in her life. She was the only professional in the family. She did not choose her mother.

Women's work for Miss Escuto included a full time job teaching special education infants and pre-schoolers. In the evening she attended classes at Grant College for her Masters degree. She was also a volunteer teacher at the church. Since Miss Escuto had her own apartment she was responsible for the care and cleaning of the premises. However, her mother cooked and brought her dinner each night. She experienced discrimination in the workplace when she mentioned to outsiders that she worked with infants. They told her that that was not a job that required skill and training; it was more like mothering.

She used the computer on her job for word-processing—to write evaluations and lesson plans. Miss Escuto majored in business education but switched careers because of the need for emotional connections. Although she changed her major to elementary education, she has expressed an interest in studying Bilingual education. Her educational choices, however, do not reflect her current position in special education.

Miss Escuto's opportunity to acquire computer knowledge began in her freshman year of high school when her class was picked at random to learn Basic—a computer language. Her male links to computer learning were her brother and cousins who were computer networking across the country. Miss Escuto eventually lost interest when the sessions with her brother and cousins became too technical. After a time gap of many years, however, her brother bought her a laptop that renewed her interest in learning about computer based technologies. She considered herself a hands-on learner who learned experientially through trial and error.

Miss Escuto thought that within the context of her family the differences between men and women who use computers were that women enjoyed the computer because it facilitated typing but men enjoyed the discussions that lasted for hours. Her nephews had Nintendo and Atari but she did not play computer games because she felt she lacked the necessary eye-hand coordination to play.

Miss Escuto had many friends from the church where she volunteered and the school where she taught who used computer based technologies. They talked about the banners, invitations, and reports produced by the computer, but they did not discuss the technical aspects of learning new programs.

Miss Escuto recognized that incredible technological changes in our society were helping to reverse gender stereotypes by giving young women new career choices. She warned however, that this breakthrough for women today was overshadowing the more basic human values. She stressed the need for emotional connections and helping others. Miss Escuto also believed that if women are to continue to progress and take the initiative they must be encouraged and praised for it.

Miss Escuto expressed dual perspectives in her thoughts about feminism. She believed in feminism and women's rights and the elimination of gender bias. But she had mixed reactions about some women with a viewpoint who were feminists. She formed her negative opinion about radical feminists who want their rights by "stomping all over and causing havoc" from the media's portrayal of "the real radical stuff." Miss Escuto recalled a phone call that exemplified discrimination in computer advertising. The salesman, who was offering computer courses, wished to speak to her husband. When she told him she did not have a husband he did not attempt to offer her the courses even though she might have been interested. He just put down the receiver.

## *Case Nine: Miss Garcia*

Miss Garcia's remembrance of childhood days revealed the young girl whose future dream was to become a teacher. Her first grade bilingual teacher was the teacher who inspired her to choose this profession. Her mother was the inspirational woman in her life; she worked at home seven days a week, night and day, to keep the family together.

Miss Garcia was graduating in June with a major in Bilingual education. However, she indicated that if she were given an alternative choice, she would probably be working in computers.

Miss Garcia's opportunity to acquire computer knowledge began in eighth grade. Her class was organized into groups of twos and each partner worked with the other to solve math computer games while learning through the experiential method. In high school she used the computer for a pre-engineering drafting course during which she created a program making and designing houses.

Miss Garcia bought a Commodore commuter from her cooperating teacher when she was a student teacher. This computer was shared at home with her brother and sisters. Sharing computer time was a block to computer learning, but Miss Garcia felt more comfortable at home than in the computer lab at Grant College. There were too many programs and too long a wait to print out the work. She never went back but preferred to use her own computer when it was available. She wanted to learn more about advanced computer programs and the use of the modem, but her Commodore was a very old model that was obsolete; this was another block to her computer learning.

Women's work for Miss Garcia included taking courses at Grant College during the day, and volunteering as a teacher in the church. She also had the responsibility of helping her mother clean the house and take care of her brother and sisters. Her brother was her male link to computer learning; he used the computer to study music at college. Interestingly, Miss Garcia believed that the treatment of girls in the family was evidence of gender discrimination. Her brothers had the opportunity to go out and date. But Miss Garcia, at the age of twenty-four, still needed permission to go out with friends.. When her father started the evening by asking her dates about their intentions Miss Garcia decided to stop dating until she moved out of the house.

Miss Garcia had many friends in high school but few friends that she could computer network with in college. Her parents encouraged her to learn about computers and her mother was willing to try to learn word-processing skills on the computer.

Miss Garcia believed that computer based technologies would result in incredible technological changes and demonstrate that we have the ability to change whatever we want and improve our world. She predicted that girls would have more choices in the future that would reverse gender stereotypes. She also believed that one day a computer would replace a teacher.

Miss Garcia expressed dual perspectives in her thoughts about feminism. She believed that women should be treated equally as men are, but she understood the man's point of view. She thought it was important for a woman to help her husband at home and also to be a working mother. She did not consider herself a feminist, but a neutral party in this debate. However, she criticized the media for their insensitive portrayal of women that resulted in the demeaning and disrespect of women that was not acceptable.

# Cross-Case Analysis

The rationale for an in-depth thematic analysis of each of the cases in this study is the importance of considering rival propositions relating to the subject of women and computer based technologies. Although the claims underlying this research are derived from feminist standpoint theory, the evidence must be examined from the alternative perspectives of each of the respondents. (Yin, 1989, p. 148) Therefore themes from the different lives of these women relating to computer based technologies were analyzed and interpreted using the alternative strategy of cross-case analysis. These multiple themes were arrayed across the six categories derived from the research questions. They were compared for pattern matching. Differences were noted and described. The evidence of the data is presented after many careful readings and reflections of the original transcripts. At the conclusion of the cross-case analysis, this researcher again considers feminist standpoint theory in order to determine if new understandings are possible relating to the lives of these professional women in education who use computer based technologies.

## Themes from Early Learning Experiences

The early beginnings of these nine women of the computer generations were strangely similar although they came from a variety of ethnic, racial, and religious backgrounds: Eight women were born in the United States; Mrs. Varsaw immigrated from Europe. The eight women born in this country remembered their early schooling experiences because of the admiration they had had for the teachers who inspired them. Three of these women remembered their early childhood teachers. Three of these women referred to teachers who inspired them when they were in public elementary schools. But Dr. Goldman referred to her elementary school teacher in the Yeshiva and Professor O'Grady, recalled the nuns who had been "inspirational of intellectual life" in high school.

Seven of these women, including Mrs. Varsaw, expressed the childhood dream of becoming a teacher. Mrs. Intel, however, wanted to be a scientist although she knew no scientists. Interestingly, seven of the women did not recall learning science or remembered science classes in which they only read about science. Miss Bell was the only respondent who described "hands-on" science lessons. Dr. Goldman stated that she wanted to be a "wanderer" and travel the world.

What were the reasons for these children's early connections to their teachers? Seven of our respondents described their emotional connections with their elementary school teachers in terms of the support, trust, and self-esteem that these teachers gave them. Professor O'Grady described her encounter with a nun, in the library in junior high school, who also awakened her to a new sense of self by associating her name with a famous Irish queen. Mrs. Varsaw remembered her elementary school teachers in Europe as strict and aloof. Although the students dared not communicate with these European teachers on a personal level, she highly respected them.

The respondents' emotional connections to their teachers endured across the expanse of many years. Positive emotional connections were also evident in the strong relationships that these women had with their mothers. Many of these mothers were not intellectual women. They were factory workers, housewives, and newly arrived immigrants who trusted and encouraged the dreams of their children. However, three of our respondents described negative mother-daughter relationships. Professor O'Grady remembered the constant berating of her mother who wanted her to stop wasting time studying. Mrs. Intel recalled: "My mother loved me but didn't inspire me because she was too passive" Mrs. Escuto revealed that her mother cooked daily meals and brought them up to her apartment because she did not live with the family. But she referred to her aunt, not her mother, as the inspirational woman in her life. Since these women had effective teacher role models whom they wished to emulate, why did six of the nine women begin their studies and careers in business?

Most of these women were limited in their choices by economic constraints and family tragedies. Professor O'Grady emphasized that there were "no choices" since her father was ill and there was no carfare to go to college. Fortunately for her students, she recognized that she was not "a policy-form person" and left the insurance company where she worked to go into teaching. Mrs. Intel was limited in her choices by family problems, illness, and death. She did not fulfill her desire to study architecture but studied computer programming so that she could obtain employment and help with the financial needs of her family.  Mrs. Varsaw's credentials as a teacher in Europe were not accepted in America, consequently she went to a technical institute to become a secretary.  Miss Lee, and Miss Escuto also majored in business studies to help with the family income although they did not feel comfortable in this environment.  Mrs. Standish was not limited in her choices during her early years because of her famous father's sports career.  But her college years were very difficult after her parent's divorce because she had to work to support herself through college.  She majored in international business and accepted a job in investment banking.

The early years of these women revealed inspirational teachers and strong emotional connections to their mothers and teachers.  But the childhood dreams of becoming teachers had to wait for many years to be fulfilled.

## *Themes from the Work Context*

The work experiences of these women were many and varied; nevertheless  seven of the nine women described aspects of discrimination that they had encountered as women in the workplace. Four of these women described verbal and financial manifestations of discrimination in the business world.  Professor O'Grady and Miss Escuto described discriminatory practices in offices and on the job at the college and pre-school level.  Interestingly, Miss Lee perceived the discrimination that she experienced in her role as elementary school teacher as age discrimination.  She thought that she was not respected because she was one of the youngest staff members.  It is to be noted that most of the respondents who worked as teachers at the elementary school level perceived no discrimination in promotions or salary, based on gender.  This may explain why Dr. Goldman whose school and work experience were at this level, stated that she never encountered discrimination on the job.  Miss Garcia was not included here because she had not graduated and did not have any previous outside work experience.  Miss Bell stated that she was appointed principal because the district office personnel were looking for a woman as a result of legislation that provided equal opportunity to women and minorities. But once on the job she stated, "women have to prove themselves more than men in leadership positions."

The awareness of discrimination in the workplace did not end at the personal level. Five of the eight respondents were acutely mindful of the unjust and discriminatory practices happening in their work environment. Professor O'Grady described the differences in computer use that she noted in schools in disadvantaged and affluent neighborhoods. Miss Bell noted that the computers in her school's computer lab were obsolete and that this would prove a disadvantage to her youngsters who lived in the inner city. Mrs. Intel described her aversion to the bigotry of the villain in the business world whose practices led her to leave the company. Mrs. Varsaw, Mrs. Intel, and Mrs. Standish noted the need for trained computer teachers in their urban elementary public and parochial schools. They realized that the children would not develop computer skills that could enable them to compete for jobs in the future by observing the computers on display in these schools.

All of the women in this study used the computer for word-processing reports, letters, etc. Mrs. Intel used the computer for statistical applications of math scores in her role as intern in a public school. Miss Bell, and Dr. Goldman used the computer to access the Internet to find funding. Miss Lee had the ability to use the computer for desk-top publishing but she had no access to computers on her job. Access was also denied to Mrs. Varsaw and Miss Escuto. Mrs. Standish, however, found no computers in the first school she taught in and "a ton of computers" in the second school she was transferred to. She noted many practical applications for computer use: teaching math through Logo, learning to use the Write to Read program, and accessing the Internet to share ideas with other teachers. Her future dream was to return to the third school she had worked in before leaving to have her baby. She was inspired by a dream to go back and set up the computer lab so that these children would have a chance to learn computer skills. Professor O'Grady expressed a similar wish to reverse discrimination and go back to teach in an elementary school where she would teach little girls not to be afraid of frogs and things.

Eight of these women who are now teaching expressed satisfaction in the job they were doing and stated that they would continue teaching even if they had the possibility of a second career choice. However, Miss Garcia who had not started on her teaching career stated that she would have loved to work with computers if she had had a second chance to choose.

These women have experienced discrimination in the workplace because they are women. They have also become sensitized to the injustice and unequal treatment of other colleagues and the children they teach. Did these professional women in education have equal access and opportunity to learn computer based technologies?

## *Themes from Opportunities to Acquire Knowledge*

These nine women of the computer generations learned to use computers at various ages and stages of their lives. Three of these women had opportunities to begin to learn computer skills while they were in the sixth grade. Miss Escuto's opportunity opened when her freshman class in high school was randomly chosen to learn BASIC, a programming language. Miss Lee, Miss Garcia, Mrs. Standish, and Miss Escuto were contemporaries at the time that computer based technologies were being introduced into the schools.

Professor O'Grady and Miss Bell learned about computers in their college years. Professor O'Grady used the mainframe for the statistical analysis of her doctoral dissertation; Miss Bell learned to operate the computer as part of a job working with literacy students at the college. Mrs. Intel, who at 48 years of age was Miss Bell's contemporary, studied computer programming after high school. She took courses in an adult education program and began her computer experience on a mainframe.

Mrs. Varsaw and Dr. Goldman recently learned to use computers. Mrs. Varsaw was introduced to computers at a technical institute while Dr. Goldman enrolled in a course in adult education. Mrs. Varsaw at the time of this study was thirty-five years of age. Dr. Goldman was fifty-three years of age; the difference of almost two decades.

Five of these women were once employed in jobs working with computers. Three of these women worked in the business world. Miss Bell and Miss Lee however, worked in the college. Dr. Goldman, Miss Garcia, Mrs. Varsaw and Miss Escuto were never employed to work with computers on the job. Interestingly, four of the five women who worked with computers on the job described a large time gap during which they stopped using computers. Miss Escuto also indicated that many years had passed before she began to use a computer again. What were the reasons for this time gap in computer learning? Finding the answer to this question began with a review of the respondents' descriptions of how they learned to use computers.

Five of the respondents said that they used logical reasoning to learn about computers. Four of the respondents said that they used intuitive reasoning to learn about computers. However, seven of the nine respondents described experiential learning methods: learning by trial and error, figuring it out, working it out, following my intuition, etc. Mrs. Intel and Mrs. Varsaw, however, learned their computer skills through formal study programs.

These respondents were motivated to learn experientially because of the need to use computers in college and on the job to write reports, evaluations, journals, etc. These were practical applications using word-processing skills. Moreover, these women were encouraged by male links to their computer learning that helped to span the time gaps in these women's computer experiences.

After many years had passed Professor O'Grady began to learn to use a desk-top computer with the help of the nice young man in the faculty computer center who came to her house to reorganize the icons on her screen. Fifteen years after Miss Bell's college computer course, she was motivated to continue to learn about the computer when her school became an ATS school. She received help from a male teacher and administrator at her school when she wanted answers to questions about her office and home computer. Miss Escuto recalled that as a teenager she no longer felt comfortable among her brother's computer friends. But it was this brother who motivated her to start learning again after many years when he bought her a laptop computer. Mrs. Standish found help from "computer nerds" working in the Economics lab when she was a college student. Many years later, she bought a computer and taught her husband how to use it. As time passed however, he began to share the "new things" that he has learned about computer programs.

Dr. Goldman and Mrs. Varsaw were also motivated to learn about computers because of practical applications on the job and at the college. Dr. Goldman hired a male student who was a computer major to tutor her so that she could add graphics to the resource guide she was writing. Mrs. Varsaw received help in accessing information for her college reports from a young boy who was her neighbor's child. Interestingly, Miss Lee stated that her uncle graduated as a computer programmer but she never spoke to him about computers. She said, "I am not one to talk about it." Professor O'Grady, Dr. Goldman, Miss Bell and Miss Escuto made the same comments. Some of these women suggested that there were differences in the way males and females learn and talk about computers.

Miss Escuto suggested that men can talk about computers for a much longer time than women can. Miss Lee indicated that women are more familiar with life experiences, not technical things like computers because they are pushed into maternal activities. Mrs. Intel observed that boys have more confidence and take chances but girls don't feel comfortable having fun. She noted that the boy high school interns were learning about the computer by playing games. The girl intern excluded herself from this type of learning. Mrs. Intel believed that "girls were more dutiful" which prevented them from learning through games.

These professional women had access and opportunity to gain computer knowledge. They had taken computer courses and described their learning methods as experiential. They were helped in these endeavors by male friends, co-workers, and family. Some of these women worked with computers in the business world and at colleges. But, their progress was not linear. There were time gaps that necessitated relearning computer skills. Although Mrs. Intel became a computer programmer, our other respondents did not have long range computer learning goals. They were motivated by more practical considerations of how the computer could aid them in their job or in their studies. Was this because there were differences in the way men and women perceive the use of computer based technologies? These women's daily lives may provide answers to this question.

## *Themes from Daily Living Experiences*

These professional women of the computer generations worked in three different settings during a twenty-four hour day. They divide their time between the home, the school and community activities. However, this distribution of time was not always predictable. Five of these women were married. Two of these women had younger children to care for. Four of these women were single but only two lived alone. All of these women indicated that they did not employ household help; they were responsible for the daily care and nurturing of the family. Two of the five married women indicated that their husbands were willing to share in certain household chores. All of these women, however, cooked, cleaned, shopped, and did the laundry for themselves and their families. The daily requirement of providing material and maternal benefits to a family is only exceeded by the demands of a job that also require responsibility for the teaching and learning of students.

Eight of these nine women worked eight or more hours a day in schools or colleges. Mrs. Standish was working in a school but is now on childcare leave. Miss Garcia was student teaching in an elementary school. Five of these women hold second jobs after school and/ or on weekends. Eight of these women were taking college or business courses in the evening to complete a degree or update their professional skills. Professor O'Grady and Dr. Goldman also indicated that they were writing text books for teachers during their spare time.

Two of these women, Miss Garcia and Miss Escuto, devoted one day a week to their church where they taught classes in religion. Mrs. Varsaw also indicated that she would soon become very active in the parochial school once her daughter entered first grade there next semester.

When do these women use computer based technologies? Five of the women who have computers at home use their computers in the very late evening and/ or on weekends. Most of the work involved the use of word-processing for reports and letters relating to their jobs. Professor O'Grady, Miss Bell, Mrs. Intel and Dr. Goldman own new multimedia computers that they use to access the Internet through America On-line. Demonstrations for family and friends usually motivated this use. Three of these women introduced their husbands to computer based technologies and were helping them with their computer work: Mrs. Standish worked one day a week at her husband's office on Microsoft Excel spreadsheets. Mrs. Intel's husband brought home his computer work from the office and she used Lotus to update his programs. Professor O'Grady had prepared a special word-processing file for the letters she has typed for her husband.

Time management is an essential factor in learning about computer based technologies. But these professional women in education had priorities: their families, their jobs, their coursework, and their church activities. When did they have the time to surf the Internet or explore the World Wide Web? How could they be challenged to reorganize their priorities so that time would be given to learning more about computer based technologies? Computer networking has been suggested as one possible strategy to achieve this objective.

## *Themes from Women Who Have Inspired Other Women*

These women of the computer generations lived in varied domains and engaged in many conversations with women throughout the course of a day's activities. In fact, Miss Bell stated, "women socialize better with other women and even men like to talk to women on that kind of level because men don't talk to each other in deep situations as easily as women tend to do." This statement while true on many levels is certainly not true when the subject is computer based technologies. Four out of the nine women described networking with female family members. Professor O'Grady communicated with five daughters. Miss Bell spoke with her aunt, cousin, and two sisters. Miss Garcia networked with two sisters and Miss Lee spoke of a sister who used computers. Four out of the nine women also networked with friends. Mrs. Intel, Mrs. Varsaw and Miss Escuto each named two friends. Mrs. Standish described one friend who used computers. Five of the nine women were able to name female workers who used computers: a colleague, a teacher, a secretary and a principal. Mrs. Varsaw was also able to name two neighbors. However, three of the nine women could not name a third women they know who used computers. Interestingly, the conversations that were described by the respondents were not about using computer based technologies or sharing new programs but they revolved around other friends and family members' experiences with computer based technologies on the job and in the home. Mrs. Intel was the only respondent who said, "I went to talk about technology and what's really happening."

Computer networking is a motivational impetus to learning. The sharing of information about computer programs and applications may result in new understandings and a continued desire to learn more. Eight of the nine professional women in education who use computer based technologies have not had the opportunity to network about new programs that would stimulate new interests. If Miss Bell was inspired by observing women she did not know, what achievements would be possible if she were linked to a network of women using computer based technologies: "I'm mesmerized when I travel by plane and see other women just whip out a laptop and get things done. They're so productive; it fascinates me."

It is significant to note that all of the nine women who use computers have family members who also use computers. Although four of the nine women networked with female family members who use computers, six of the nine women networked with male family members. Mrs. Intel and Dr. Goldman have sons who used computers on their jobs; Mrs. Varsaw and Miss Escuto networked with brothers while Mrs. Standish networked with her husband. Thus evidently family contextual support for learning is an important factor in the culture of these women who use computer based technologies.

The theme of computer networking surfaces again in the respondents' predictions on the effects of computer based technologies on students in the classrooms of today and tomorrow.

## *Themes from Thoughts about the Effects of Computer Based Technologies on Students*

These nine women professional educators of the computer generations described incredible technological changes that would result in future years, but they were very concerned about the present and future negative effects of computer based technologies on students.

Eight out of our nine respondents warned of the sedentary, addictive and isolated lifestyles of students whose time was spent alone playing with computer games. Mrs. Standish also foresaw the importance of monitoring access to the Internet by teachers, parents, and government officials so that the children would not have access to programs containing inappropriate material. Eight of the nine respondents emphasized the need for emotional connections to other children in the lives of their students.

Eight of these nine women also agreed that the emotional connection provided by the interaction of student and teacher was the primary reason computers would never replace teachers. Mrs. Varsaw also suggested that the teacher's role was not only to socialize children but also to teach beliefs. Miss Garcia however, thought that computers would replace teachers in the next twenty-five years.

All of our respondents described the fast pace of living that will be accelerated by computer based technologies in the future. Moreover, they all agreed that the choices presented to girls would be greater in the future in terms of career choices that would reverse present day gender stereotypes. However, two of our respondents warned of the great rift between women who were computer literate and those who were not. Dr. Goldman stated, "The effect of computer technology would be to create more of an upper and lower class." Mrs. Varsaw predicated that competition would be "terrible for jobs" in the future and that girls who did not have computer skills would have "very difficult lives." Interestingly, Professor O'Grady and Miss Lee shared the hope that computer based technologies would give women and men the choice of working at home rather than in offices to "free up" time and "do the family thing."

Computer networking was discussed by two of our respondents. Mrs. Standish saw computers as "an incredible resource linking schools across the country so that teachers can share ideas." Principal Bell, however, suggested more "fantastic" changes in her prediction that one day our children will be communicating by computers with someone on another planet.

Miss Escuto observed that there was a "breakthrough for women today." Women students were taking initiative, making choices, and succeeding in fulfilling their dreams. She cautioned however, that they needed to be "praised" and supported in these endeavors.

This concludes the cross-sectional analysis of the themes that have compared the responses of women of the computer generations for similarities and differences. The next section will focus on Feminist Standpoint theory as a basis for analysis of the narratives of these nine women who use computer based technologies.

## *Focusing the Lenses of Feminist Standpoint Theory*

Feminist Standpoint Theory, which has been grounded in the claims of Harding (1991), will be employed in this section in an attempt to shed new light on the narratives of these women who use computer based technologies. Claim one suggests that valuing women's daily life experiences in research studies will provide new insights because women's perspectives are unique. They have been shaped and constrained by life experiences determined by their gender.

These women's early learning experiences, viewed from the feminist perspective, began with their socialization as girls according to predetermined patterns of the sex-gender system. The attachment to their mothers and female teachers may be seen as evidence of women's relational personality structures that conform to the pattern of female not male. Conformity to cultural stereotypes was also evident in the respondents' descriptions of childhood games: playing house and school. This training of the female in preparation for future roles as housewife, mother, and teacher also extended to learned patterns of thought such as empathy and sensitivity to the needs of others, which must be given priority over one's own needs. However, three of our respondents in this study describe events that did not conform to this cultural pattern: Professor O'Grady, Mrs. Intel, and Miss Escuto refused to recognize their mothers as role models. Interestingly, these three women also stated that their choices of careers were independent decisions that were not influenced by others.

The early learning experiences of these women in elementary school also varied. Three of these girls, Miss Lee, Miss Garcia, and Mrs. Standish had opportunities to learn about computers in sixth grade. Miss Escuto was introduced to computers in her freshman year of high school. Feminist standpoint theory would assert that the political changes that occurred as a result of the Feminist Revolution changed the curricula in many schools and opened up opportunities in science, math, and technology once reserved for boys. However, this was not true of the elementary science curricula. Eight of the nine respondents, whose ages spanned over forty years, reported the same findings: their science classes consisted of lectures or the reading from a text. This did not generate an interest in science. Mrs. Intel, whose childhood dream was to become a scientist, recalled "Nada, zip, nothing" about her science elementary science classes. These girls were not motivated to engage in experiential science learning in elementary school.

Feminist standpoint theory states that women are strangers in the world of business that is dominated by the values and beliefs of men in power. The oppression experienced by women who have chosen to leave the home for a career in the business world is well documented in the narratives of women of the computer generations. Our respondents who majored in business or worked in the world of business reported incidents involving sex discrimination. Many of the respondents also described feelings of not belonging in the world of business. For example, Professor O'Grady's commented, "I am not a policy form person so I left insurance to go into teaching." Miss Lee stated, "I couldn't see myself sitting in an office for the rest of my life" Mrs. Intel whose first career was as a computer programmer felt compelled to leave two positions because of her reluctance to be a part of the prejudice and discriminatory practices that were prevalent in the workplace.

However, it is significant that six of the nine women who majored in business or worked in the world of business had the opportunities to use computer based technologies in college courses and in their careers. This was most important because these experiences not only introduced

Mrs. Intel, Miss Bell, and Mrs. Varsaw to computers but also closed the learning gap of Miss Lee and Mrs. Standish who were introduced to computers in elementary school.

Feminist standpoint theory describes the subordinated status of women in the family. All of the women in our study were responsible for household chores. Mrs. Intel was the only respondent who indicated that her husband shared equally in household tasks. Eight of our respondents worked outside the home for eight or more hours a day. Professor O'Grady, Miss Bell, and Miss Lee reported that they have other jobs in the late afternoon and evening. Miss Escuto and Miss Garcia also devote one evening a week to teaching in the church. Two of these women, Mrs. Standish and Mrs. Varsaw, also care for very young children. Miss Garcia and Miss Lee, although not married, care for younger brothers and sisters. The subordinated status of women obligates them to accept these responsibilities as natural. The time that is needed to learn about computer based technologies must be taken out of these very long and busy days. But since this time is devoted to personal growth it does not take priority over family, work, college, and church. Therefore one of the major problems for women in learning to use computer based technologies is isolating the time to learn.

Feminist standpoint theory also stated that women experience battle gains and losses in this age of science in transition. These women's use of computer based technologies may be considered "gains" in a society where women's place was in the home. But the "losses" are also recognizable in terms of limitations of computer access and opportunity. Professor O'Grady had no access to computer based technologies in her office or in the college classrooms where she teaches the future teachers of tomorrow. Mrs. Intel, who was a former computer programmer, worked on a word-processing program in the science lab at Grant College. Why was this woman who has such capabilities not been asked to work with students who need to develop their computer skills? Miss Bell was the principal of a school and an adjunct professor whose classes meet at her school in the evenings. If her school had computers with access to the Internet she could have had her elementary school students and staff learning computer skills during the day and her college students developing stategies to teach curriculum via the Internet in the evenings. Mrs. Varsaw, Miss Lee, and Mrs. Standish no longer have access to computers at home and therefore have no opportunities to extend their computer knowledge. These three women are teachers in elementary schools but their computer learning is not recognized or utilized for the benefit of the children or the staff. Miss Escuto and Miss Garcia have often expressed interest in learning more about computers. But Miss Escuto is limited by her laptop which does not have Windows or a modem. Miss Garcia has a Commodore that is already obsolete. Dr. Goldman, Miss Bell, and Professor O'Grady have state of the art computers at home. But they need the time and the incentive to explore the Internet and the World Wide Web.

Feminist standpoint theory supports a feminist perspective in a world of great technological changes. Although all of our respondents recognized the importance of the feminist revolution for women's rights, only three of our respondents considered themselves feminists. Five of our respondents did not like the limitations imposed on their choices by feminists. Interestingly, most of our respondents had dual perspectives on the feminist perspective. As women with daughters they wanted these advantages for their girls, but as women with husbands, brothers, and sons, they recognized the importance of maintaining the status quo.

## Chapter VI

# Conclusions, Significance, and Recommendations

## *Conclusions*

Feminist standpoint theory, in this study, has focused attention on the lives of nine professional women in education who use computer based technologies. It has revealed the importance of listening to women as they reflect upon their life experiences and computer based technologies. Feminist standpoint theory has provided an alternative perspective on the priorities that women have, on their use of time, and on their opportunities and access to computer based technologies. Feminist Standpoint theory has highlighted the discrimination these women have experienced in the workplace. However, this study has also revealed the supportive relationships of men who have forged links to women that have helped them to learn about computer based technologies. Feminist Standpoint theory has suggested the importance of valuing women's lives. This research, based on that premise, has produced significant understandings relating to the original research questions.

## Early Learning Experiences

The early learning experiences of these women affected their use of computer based technologies in three distinct ways. Their early training at home and in school focused on the care and nurturance of others. This was evident in the games they played, the careers they chose, and the role models they followed. The pattern of thinking that resulted from this training centered women's thoughts on family, work, and community activities as the first priorities in their lives. Personal growth and development were assigned a second place.

The early education of these women reflected the stereotypical beliefs about females in our society. Science and math classes involving experiential learning were not available for most of these women in elementary school. In fact, their early educational experiences did not provide these respondents as young girls with role models other than female teachers. Moreover, many of the elementary school teachers inspired these women to follow similar careers through the strong emotional connections made in childhood.

The early introduction of these women to computers was sporadic reflecting a lack of planning and defining of long range goals. Three of the students introduced to computers in the sixth grade were given cursory learning experiences by teachers who were not trained. Sometimes one computer was available for an entire class to use and on other occasions five or six children shared one computer. However, these three students were fortunate to be at that juncture of time and place when computers were introduced into the school setting.

## The Work Context and Opportunities to Acquire Knowledge

These women have described their work context and its relationship to computer based technologies in terms of preparation, access, and opportunity to learn and to use computer based technologies.

Respondents who started their studies as business majors were taught computer skills. Those respondents who began their careers in business also had access and opportunity to use computers in the workplace and they were encouraged to continue learning on the job. However, the discrimination they experienced as women in the business world and their need for emotional connections were decisive factors in their decision to leave business to become teachers.

Respondents who entered the Graduate Program in Education at Grant College were offered courses in Word-processing, Logo, and Desktop Publishing. They also had access to the computer lab; however, most of these women did not take advantage of this opportunity because they were uncomfortable in this setting.

Respondents who worked in schools and colleges expressed frustration at not having access to computers in the classrooms where they taught. The principal in this study did have access to a computer in her office. Moreover, the senior professor in this study was not given an office computer although she expressed a definite need for one. However, she did have access to the faculty computer lab and to a computer programming course offered by the college.

## Daily Living Experiences

These women described their daily living experiences within the context of the family and its relationship to computer based technologies. They discussed access, opportunity, and male links to learning.

Access to computer based technologies at home varied. Four respondents owned state of the art computers, two respondents owned obsolete models and three respondents were unable to purchase computers because of financial considerations.

Opportunity to use computer based technologies at home were limited for all respondents because of the time devoted to their family, their jobs, their coursework and their community activities that had first priority. Therefore, time gaps were evident in their computer learning experiences because in the busyness of their daily lives these emotional connections held preeminence.

Male links to computer learning in the family were described by six of the respondents in this study. These women connected to brothers, sons, and husbands who motivated and shared their interests in computer based technologies. Interestingly, three of the respondents' husbands were introduced to computers by their wives who used their computer knowledge to help their husbands in work relating to their jobs.

## Inspirational Others

These women described networking with other women who use computer based technologies in the neighborhood, the office, the school, and the church. Interestingly, while these women shared with other women the concerns and life experiences of family and friends relating to computer based technologies, the shared knowledge of technical aspects of using computers was usually discussed with men. The reason for this may be attributed to the male teachers, brothers, sons, and colleagues who supported them in their computer learning experiences. However, most of these women described experiential learning methods as they explored computer software programs: learning by trial and error, figuring it out, working it out, following my intuition, etc.

## *Effects of Computer Based Technologies*

These professional women in education described positive and negative effects of computer based technologies on the students in their classrooms of today. They also predicted incredible technological changes in society and in the life styles of students of the next generation resulting from the use of computer based technologies.

They emphasized the importance of computers for word-processing reports, evaluations, and journals in classrooms today. Specific computer programs such as Write To Read and Logo were considered meaningful alternatives to traditional learning materials. Telecommunications including the ability to access the Internet, engage in chat sessions, and share ideas through NYCNET were highlighted as examples of positive effects of computer based technologies.

These women also warned of the sedentary, addictive and isolated lifestyles of students whose time was spent alone playing computer games for many hours during a day. They saw the need to regulate and monitor computer on-line programs with adult content so that students would have access to appropriate rather than indecent information. They also emphasized that computer based technologies could not substitute for the emotional connections to other students and teachers that must be made if the educational community is to survive.

These women predicted an even faster pace of living that will be accelerated by computer based technologies in the future. They predicted many new choices for girls who were computer literate that would reverse gender discrimination and create new work options. However, they saw a great rift between girls who have computer skills and those who do not which would lead to the division of society into stratified classes based on the criteria of computer literacy. Some women predicted incredible technological changes in a world where a student would communicate with someone on another planet. These changes are beginning now!

# *Significance*

In today's information society computer literacy is no longer an option. Educators need to prepare their students to function in a world where distance learning and telecommunications are now accessible. This technological revolution is changing the future of teaching and learning. Hand held digital assistants, E-mail, and desk top conferencing have transformed our ways of communicating. Netscape and other Internet navigational tools are simplifying access to the World Wide Web by providing a graphic interface for users through still pictures, motion pictures and sound.

This proliferation of computer technology requires opportunities for women to access computer training. Classrooms and computer labs in some schools now have computers with multimedia capabilities: CD-ROM drives, Sound cards, and modems. Teachers are using new computer software programs that feature full screen, full motion video that simulate field trips. Photos and animation add to interactive experiences in these programs.

Students and teachers are creating new types of learning materials through HyperCard, Photoshop, cameras, scanners, and other computer reference materials. They are learning to design and create their own multimedia experiences.

Computers are the tools of the future. In this information age where computer based technologies are changing every aspect of our daily lives, it is imperative that professional women in education be computer literate. Young women must be trained in this field without the onus of considering it a male domain.

# *Recommendations*

Women need equal access to computer based technologies beginning in their early learning experiences. Computers should be available for use in early childhood classrooms where time to learn computer skills is programmed into the school day. Computers should be used in conjunction with lessons in science, social studies, math, and so on.

Career days in elementary schools should involve visits to offices in corporations and higher educational institutions where female students can see women working and using computer based technologies in many different occupations.

Computer magazines and newspapers that contain advertisements that promote the use of computers need to portray women who use computers in power roles. Publishing companies need to be sensitized to the affects their advertisements have on girls growing up in the computer age.

Workshops in telecommunications should be made mandatory for teachers as part of staff and grade conferences so that they can get a jump start on exploring the Internet and World Wide Web while they are in computer labs in their own schools.

Stipends and time should be made available for the computer training of women professionals who are in educational leadership positions so that they can motivate and influence other women to use computer based technologies. These training sessions need to be taught by teams of male and female instructors.

Mothers need to be invited into schools where they can see their youngsters learning to use computers. These visits may take place in computer labs during the school day or in after school computer clubs. This will encourage parents to purchase a computer for their home and provide an opportunity for administrators to set up workshops for parents who want to learn the fundamentals of computer based technologies.

Colleges that have graduate programs in education need to have computers in classes studying advanced teaching methods. These computers should be available in a ratio of one computer to one student. They should be linked to on-line telecommunications services so that those graduate students who are teachers can experience hands-on computer lab sessions after their in school work day.

Partnerships among schools, businesses and government agencies should be set up for on-line conferencing in order to promote the computer work skills that will be needed by students. The materials developed from these conferences need to be included in the curriculum of K-12 students.

Interactive computer simulations are important for promoting women students' involvement in professional development opportunities. These programs would permit students to experience different occupational roles that would give them more occupational choices early in their learning experience.

Colleges should offer courses for future teachers that demonstrate how to link K-12 classrooms to community resources, i.e., museums, hospitals, libraries, etc., using computer based technologies. In the future female students will be motivated to explore shopping centers and other virtual worlds using the electronic representations, "avatars," of their own faces "Seated at a personal computer equipped with a video camera, a video image of the user can be moved through an electronic replication of a store, a bank, or other environment, simulating such activities as shopping, banking, or even hiking in the mountains" (Flynn, 1996, March 4, p. D3).

Live links to experts using computer based technologies would not only stimulate the interests of all students in current educational topics, but may motivate young women to pursue new careers in natural history, photography, and so on as they interact with these experts in chat sessions.

On-site school competitions such as electronic debates will provide another opportunity to use computer based technologies. This would enable teams of students to work together to solve problems relating to conflict resolution. E-mail could be used to transmit decisions and promote cooperative decision-making. This would provide an opportunity for girls to interact with boys in gaining participatory decision-making skills relating to real life experiences.

Interactive multimedia—a system that responds to signals from the user by changing the content or pace of instruction—should be part of the new curriculum in Language Arts, Social Studies, and the Sciences. This will capture the attention of all students and encourage critical thinking skills. Moreover, presentations in science would be accessible to female students and augment the traditional lectures and lab sessions.

Computer based technologies used in colleges and classrooms should emphasize non-competitive long range goals so that women can continue to learn without time gaps in their learning. This environment should encourage cooperative learning and provide opportunities for emotional connections that support computer networking.

## *Future Research*

Feminist standpoint theory asserts that women's lives have been neglected and devalued as starting points for research. Therefore I chose nine professional women in education who use computer based technologies for this study. However, the research findings from this study are limited in number, setting, and time. This study needs to be replicated in the larger population. Collaborative research teams of women researchers might visit other schools in inner cities and suburbs to compare the findings in this study with studies of other women educators, i.e., superintendents, principals, and teachers. The respondent group should include women executives, engineers, secretaries and office workers who use computer based technologies.

Parallel studies of men who use computer based technologies are needed to compare their responses to the interview questions. It would be interesting to compare their responses to the thematic photographs that were used as a stimulus for discussion to determine their views relating to feminist standpoint theory claims.

Researchers might take their own photographs to further enhance the cluster categories in order to provide more specific data on other components of the clusters. For example the cluster category "strangers" might be exemplified using a photograph of women and computers in the classroom setting. This photograph would be used as a stimulus for discussion about computers in the school environment.

Further research is needed to determine if other woman value women's opinions, advice, or experiences relating to computer based technologies in education. Is gender stereotyping perpetuated by women who value only men's ideas about computer based technologies?

Research is needed to study the use of computer based technologies in elementary schools. Quantitative data on the number of computers, modems and telephone lines per school should be augmented by qualitative data on the learning styles of male and female students who use computers. Is experiential learning favored by females? Do women like to learn in cooperative learning groups or individually? What type of training is given to teachers who use computer based technologies?

Time management studies are needed to assess the time women devote to work in the home and out of the home, coursework, and community activities. What impact does this have on women's learning about computer based technologies?

Qualitative studies are needed to determine if women college students in education use computer labs. If so, what is the frequency of their use? What training sessions are available and at what hours? Do women teach these training sessions or tutor in computer labs? What types of software programs do women use? What types of software programs do they want available?

Studies of professional women in education who use computer based technologies should be followed up by focus groups in which the respondents share ideas. The narratives in this study were fascinating, but unfortunately they were never shared by the nine respondents due to the confidentiality requirement. Shared narratives may stimulate new insights into women's thoughts about the knowledge claims of feminist standpoint theory.

Finally, the importance of valuing women's lives suggests the need to record the educational experiences of women from many different cultures. These stories will not only reveal the patterns of discrimination, which feminists would refer to as the history of oppression, but will also demonstrate the progress made for children to read and women to remember. The sharing of these stories will value women's knowledge and inspire new possibilities in the dreams of our children.

Studies of the lives of professional women in education who use computer based technologies may provide the catalyst that will provoke other women to network and share their experiences using this technology in schools and in their daily lives. Our society is dependent on the full development of human resources for economic growth and future prosperity. This potential talent cannot be lost because of the subtle exclusion of women from learning and teaching about computer based technologies.

# *Appendix A*

# Sample Informed Consent Form

Dear Participant,

Hope Morritt is a doctoral student in the department of Educational Administration at New York University. She is presently engaged in a research study about the lives of professional women in education who use computer based technologies.

Respondents will be asked to engage in a series of three interviews to obtain data for this study. Confidentiality will be maintained for all respondents involved in this study. Information received during the interviews will be coded so that there will be no link to the respondent's identity. Keys to the code will be maintained separately.

Participation in this study is voluntary. The third interview will consist of a dialogue in which the participant can react to the researcher's understandings of the previous two interviews. If you are interested in participating in this study please sign the consent statement below. Thank you.

Date_____

I, _____ have read and agreed to the above information and I am willing to participate in three or more *taped* interview sessions for the study about women and computer based technologies. I understand that I have the right to review all or any portion of these audiotapes and request that it be destroyed. I understand that I have the right to withhdraw from this study at any time.

_____
Signature

# *Appendix B*

# Interview Guide

## *Photograph One*

The thematic lens of "Valuing Women's Experiences" is central to photograph one. Clusters relating to this theme are used to formulate the probes. *See page 16 for specific clusters relating to each thematic lens.*

*Please look at the two cartoons on page one.*

**Probe**: Please explain why you do or don't agree with the artist's viewpoint: that women are more knowledgeable than men about computers?

**Probe**: What subjects do you think women are more knowledgeable about?

**Probe**: What is your opinion about the cartoon character's statement about women's intuition?

**Probe**: Do you consider your reasoning more intuitively oriented or logically oriented? Why?

**Probe**: What effect do you think this has had on your learning about computers?

## *Photograph Two*

The thematic lens of "Strangers" is the main focus of page two. Clusters relating to this theme are used to formulate the probes.

*Please look at the photograph on page two.*

**Probe**: What do you remember about your science classes in elementary school?

**Probe**: When you were little, what did you want to be when you grew up?

**Probe**: What or who influenced your present choice of the career you now have?

**Probe**: If you had a second chance to choose, what would you be doing today?

## Photograph Three

The thematic lens of "Oppression/Knowledge" is the main focus of this page. Clusters relating to this theme are used to formulate the probes.

*Please look at the photograph on page three.*

**Probe**: What do you think the role of the women is in this office?

**Probe**: Whose two hands are in the foreground of the picture?

**Probe**: Have you ever had or been offered a job working with computers? Tell me about it.

**Probe**: Can you relate an experience illustrating how being a woman has affected your career?

## Photograph Four

The thematic lens of "Battle Gains and Losses" is the main focus of page four. Clusters relating to this theme are used to formulate the probes.

*Please look at the photograph on page four.*

**Probe**: Which woman in this photograph would you like to be? Why?

**Probe**: Why did you want to learn about computers?

**Probe**: Did you experience any difficulties in your initial orientation to computers? Tell me about it. (How long ago was this?)

**Probe**: What or who motivated you to continue to learn about computer based technologies?

**Probe**: What computer based technologies have you used? (Modems, fax, LAN networking, etc.)

**Probe**: How have your friends and coworkers responded to your use of computer based technologies?

## Photograph Five

The thematic lens of "Women's Work" is the main focus of photograph five. Clusters relating to this theme are used to formulate the probes.

*Please look at the photograph on page 5.*

**Probe**: Why do you think this woman is a working mother?

**Probe**:  When do you think this woman uses the computer in her home?

**Probe**:  What responsibilities do you have at work and in your home?

**Probe**:  How do family members in your house share in housework and other responsibilities around the home?

**Probe**:  When do you find time to use computer based technologies?

## Photograph Six

The thematic lens of "Accepting Differences" is the main focus of photograph six. Clusters relating to this theme are used to formulate the probes.

*Please look at the photograph on page six.*

**Probe**:  What is the relationship of the woman and the girl in this picture?

**Probe**:  Why is the woman concentrating on the girl?

**Probe**:  Can you describe three women in your life who use computers? (Ascertain race, class, education, and relationship to interviewee)

## Photograph Seven

The thematic lens of "Theory and Science in Transition" is the main focus of photograph seven. Clusters relating to this theme are used to fomulate the probes.

*Please look at the photograph on page seven.*

**Probe**:  What is your answer to the question on this page.

**Probe**:  Can you describe some positive effects of computer based technologies in your role as an educator?

**Probe**:  Can you describe some negative effects of computer based technologies in your role as an educator?

**Probe**:  What are your predictions for the future of this little girl in the picture in relation to computer based technologies and education, career, and life style in the next 25 years?

# *Appendix C*

# **Sample of Audit Trail Log**

**March 7, 1995** Ms. Varsaw called me again this morning . She explained that she was eager to participate in the interview sessions and asked me to reschedule the interviews. I asked her to contact me as soon as she felt better.

I spent a great deal of time listening to the tapes and reading the transcribed interviews. Themes leap from the pages. Now I understand the importance of coding. As I develop the coded themes, I realize that several respondents have not discussed important issues. I am now taking notes to prepare for the next interview session.

**March 8, 1995** I continue to develop the codes for interview one. It amazes me that each time I think I am finished, a new category emerges. If these are the descriptive codes, what will the interpretative codes be like?

**March 10, 1995** *Quantitative data:* There are 147 pages in my first round of 8 interviews. Descriptive Codes: Thirteen main code categories from this first round and 70 descriptive codes in total. I see more! But I must stop to develop the infobase in Folio Views for searching.

**March 11, 1995** After two months away from Folio Views, I have returned to this program to develop an infobase. Long hours have been spent converting the transcripts on Word 5 discs from Margaret to Microsoft Word 2.0 format. Steps involved: Open file. Choose Drive B. Select file to be opened. Click. Choose Edit from the Menu. Choose Select All from that menu. Then select COPY from the same menu. *(Change margins using Page Setup under Format in menu. Choose Print Preview under File menu to align pages. Insert Page numbers.)* Choose New from File Menu. Choose Paste from Edit Menu. The new version of the file should now be on the screen. ***Important***: Choose Save As from the File Menu and Choose Drive C. Test to see if you have it on the hard drive by removing the disc from the external drive. Choose the file you have copied. If all goes well you should see it on the screen. Do this for each file on the disc.

Ironically, the meticulous attention needed to convert the files have paid off. The Folio Views Manual seems easier to understand! I need to use Create to develop a Production File. This program is available in the IBM version of Folio.

# Appendix D

# Thematic Photographs
## (One Through Seven)

### Photograph One

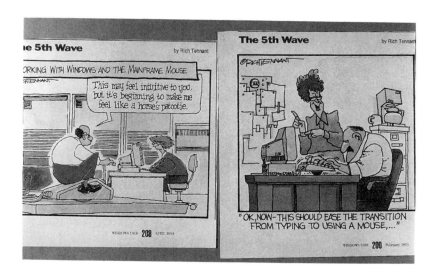

## *Photograph Two*

## *Photograph Three*

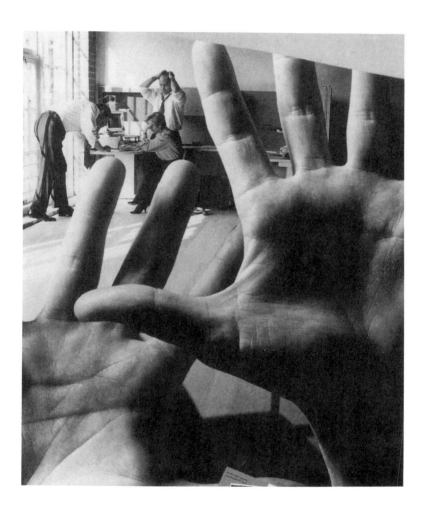

*Appendix D*

## *Photograph Four*

# *Photograph Five*

*Appendix D*

# *Photograph Six*

## *Photograph Seven*

# Bibliography

Anderson, R. E. (1987). Females surpass males in computer problem solving: Findings from the Minnesota Computer Literacy Assessment. *Journal of Educational Computing Research, 3*, 39-51.

Aptheker, B. (1989). *Tapestries of life: Women's work, women's consciousness, and the meaning of daily experience*. Amherst: The University of Massachusetts Press.

Arenz, B.W., & Lee M. (1990). Gender differences in the attitude, interest and participation of secondary students in computer use. Paper presented at the annual meeting of the American Educational Research Association, Boston, MA.

Arpad, S. S. (1992). The personal cost of the feminist knowledge explosion. In C. Kramarae & D. Spender (Eds.), *The knowledge explosion: Generations of feminist scholarship* (pp. 333-339). New York: Teachers College Press.

Bogdan, R. C., & Biklen, S. K. (1992). *Qualitative research for education* (2nd ed.). Boston: Allyn and Bacon.

Bordo, S. (1986). *The Cartesian masculinization of thought and culture*. Albany: State University of New York Press.

Bowers, C. A. (1988). *The cultural dimensions of educational computing: Understanding the non-neutrality of technology*. New York: Teachers College Press.

Brownell, G. (1993). Macintosh clip art: Are females and minorities represented? *Journal of Research on Computing in Education, 26*, 116-121.

Bunster, X. (1977). Talking pictures: Field method and visual mode. *Signs: Journal of Women in Culture and Society, 2*, 278-293.

Collis, B. (1985). Psychsocial implications of sex differences in attitudes toward computers: Results of a survey. *International Journal of Women's Studies, 8*, 207-213.

Damarin, S. K. (1991). Rethinking science and mathematics curriculum and instruction: Feminist perspectives in the computer era. *Journal of Education, 173*, 107-123.

Duffy, T., & Berchelmann T. (1995). *Computing Concepts*. Belmont: Wadsworth Publishing Company.

Eccles, J. S., & Jacobs, J. (1986). Social Forces shape math participation. *Signs, II*, 367-380.

Eccles, J. S. (1989). Bringing young women to math and science. In M Crawford & M. Gentry (Eds.), *Gender and thought: Psychological perspectives* (pp. 36-58). New York: Springer-Verlag.

Edwards, P. (1990). The army and the microworld: Computers and the politics of gender identity. *Signs: Journal of Women in Culture and Society, 16*, 102-127.

Ely, M (1991). *Circles within circles*. New York: The Falmer Press.

Flynn, L. (1996, March 4). *The New York Times*, p. D3.

Gergen, K. J. (1988). Feminist critique of science and the challenge of social epistemology. In M. M. Gergen (ed.), *Feminist thought and the structure of knowledge* (pp. 27-48). New York: New York University Press.

Gilligan, C. (1982). *In a different voice: Psychological theory and women's development*. Cambridge: Harvard University Press.

Glaser, B.G., & Strauss, A.L. (1967). *The discovery of grounded theory*. Chicago: Aldine.

Harding, S. (1983). Why has the sex/gender system become visible only now? In S. Harding & M. B. Hintikka (Eds.), *Discovering reality: Feminist perspectives on epistomology, metaphysics, methodology, and philosophy of science* (pp. 311-324). Boston: D. Reidel Publishing Company.

Harding, S. (Ed.). (1987a). *Feminism and methodology*. Bloomington: Indiana University Press.

Harding, S. (1987b). The instability of the analytical categories of feminist theory. In S. Harding & J. O'Barr (Eds.), *Sex and scientific inquiry* (pp. 283-302). Chicago: The University of Chicago Press.

Harding, S. (1989a). Feminist justificatory strategies. In A. Gary & M. Pearsall (Eds.), *Women, knowledge, and reality: explorations in feminist philosophy* (pp. 189-201). Boston: Unwin Hyman.

Harding, S. (1989b). Is there a feminist method? In N. Tuana (Ed.), *Feminism & science* (pp. 17-32). Bloomington: Indiana University Press.

Harding, S. (1991). *Whose science? Whose knowledge? Thinking from women's lives*. New York: Cornell University Press.

Harrington, H. L. (1993). The essence of technology and the education of teachers. *Journal of Teacher Education, 44*, 5-15.

Hartsock, N. C. M. (1983). The feminist standpoint: developing the ground for a specifically feminist historical materialism In S. Harding & M.B. Hintikka (Eds.), *Discovering reallity: Feminist perspectives on epistomology, metaphysics, methodology, and philosophy of science* (pp. 311-324). Boston: D.Reidel Publishing Company.

Hess, R. D. & Miura, I. T. (1985). Gender differences in enrollment in computer camps and classes. *Sex Roles, 13*, 193-203.

Hines, M. (1982). Prenatal gonadal hormones and sex differences in human behavior. *Psychological Bull. 92*, 56-80.

Honey, M. & Henriquez, A. (1993). *Telecommunications and K-12 educators: Findings from a national survey*. New York: Bank Street College of Education.

Kay, R. (1992a) An analysis of methods used to examine gender differences in computer-related behavior. *Journal of Educational Computing Research, 8*, 277-291.

Kay, R. (1992b). Understanding gender differences in computer attitudes, aptitude, and use: An invitation to build theory. *Journal of Research on Computing in Education, 25*, 159-171.

Kay, R. (1993). A critical evaluation of gender differences in computer-related behavior. *Computers in the Schools*, *9*, 81-93.

Kay, R. (1994a). Understanding and evaluating measures of computer ability: Making a case for an alternative metric. *Journal of Research on Computing in Education*, *26*, 270-284.

Kay, R. (1994b). Charting pathways of conceptual change in the use of computer software: A formative analysis. *Journal of Research on Computing in Education*, *26*, 403-417.

Keller, E. F. (1982). Feminism and science. *Signs: Journal of women in culture and society*, *7*, 589-602.

Keller, E. F. (1985). *Reflections on gender and science*. New Haven: Yale University Press.

Kiesler, S., Sproull, L., & Eccles, J. (1985). Poolhalls, chips, and war games: Women in the culture of computing. *Psychology of Women Quarterly*, *9*, 451-462.

Kramer, P., & Lehman, S. (1990) Mismeasuring women: A critique of research on computer ability and avoidance. *Signs: Journal of Women in Culture and Society*, *16*, 159-173.

Levi-Strauss, C. (1968). *The savage mind*. Chicago: University of Chicago Press

Lincoln, Y. S., & Guba, E. G. (1985). *Naturalistic inquiry*. Newbury Park: Sage Publications.

Lincoln, Y. S. (1990). The making of a constructivist. In E. G. Guba (Ed.), *The paradign dialog*. (pp. 67-87). Newbury Park: Sage Publications.

Lorde, A. (1984). *Sister/Outsider*. Trumansburg, N.Y.: The Crossing Press.

Loyd, B. H., & Gressard C. (1984). *Computer attitudes: Differences by gender and amount of computer experience*. Paper presented at the annual meeting of the American Educational Research Association, New Orleans, L.A.

Makrakis, V. (1992). Gender and computing in schools in Japan: The "we can, I can't" paradox. *Computers and Education*, *20*, 191-198.

Markus, M., & Oyserman, D. (1989). Gender and thought: The role of the self concept. In M. Crawford & M. Gentry (Eds.), *Gender and thought: Psychological perspectives* (pp. 100-122). New York: Springer-Verlag.

Marshall, C., & Rossman, R. B. (1989). *Designing qualitative research*. Newbury Park: Sage Publications.

Martin, D. C., Heller, R. S., & Mahmoud, E. (1992). American and Soviet children's attitudes toward computers. *Journal of Educational Computing Research*. *8*, 155-185.

McCracken, G. (1988). *The long interview*. Newbury Park: Sage Publications.

McGrath, D., Thurston, L. P., McLellan, H., Stone, D., & Tischhauser, M. (1992). Sex differences in computer attitudes and beliefs among rural middle school children after a teacher training intervention. *Journal of Research on Computing in Education*, *24*, 469-485.

McInerney,V., McInerney, D. & Sinclair, K. (1994). Student teachers, computer anxiety, and computer experience. *Journal of Educational Computing Research*, *11*, 27-50.

Miles, M. B., & Huberman, A. M. (1984). *Qualitative data analysis A sourcebook of new methods.* Beverly Hills: Sage Publications.

Miles, M. B., & Huberman, A. M. (1994). *Quantitative data analysis An expanded sourcebook.* (2nd edition) Thousand Oaks: Sage Publications.

Millman, M., & Kanter, R. M. (1987) Introduction to another voice: Feminist perspectives on social life and social science. In S. Harding (Ed.), *Feminism and methodology.* (pp. 29-36) Bloomington: Indiana University Press.

Ogletree, S. M. & Williams, S. W. (1990). Sex and sex-typing effects on computer attitudes and aptitude. *Sex Roles, 11/12,* 703-712.

Okebukola, P. A. (1993). The gender factor in computer anxiety and interest among some Australian high school students. *Educational Research, 35,* 181-188.

Patton, M. Q. (1980). *Qualitative evaluation and research methods.* Beverly Hills: Sage Publications.

Patton, M. Q. (1990). *Qualitative evaluation and research methods* (2nd ed.). Newbury Park: Sage Publications.

Pfaffenberger, B. (1988). *Microcomputer applications in qualitative research.* Newbury Park: Sage Publications.

Reinen, I. J., & Plomp, T. (1993). Some gender issues in educational computer use: Results of an international comparative survey. *Computers and Education, 20,* 353-365.

Rock, D., Ekstrom, R., Goertz, M., Pollack, J., & Hilton, T. (1985). A study of excellence in high school education: Longitudinal study, 1980-1982. Unpublished report. In B. Gutek & T. Bikson, Differential experiences of men and women in computerized offices. *Sex Roles, 13,* 123-135 as cited in Vernon-Gerstenfeld.

Sacks, C. H., Bellisimo, Y. & Mergendoller, J. (1994). Attitudes toward computers and computer use: The issue of gender. *Journal of Research on Computing in Education, 26,* 256-269.

Scheingold, K., Hawkins, J., & Char, C. (1984). "I'm the thinkest, you're the typist" : The interaction of technology and the social life of classrooms. *Journal of Social Issues, 40,* 49-61.

Shakeshaft, C. (1987). *Women in educational administration.* Newbury Park: Sage Publications.

Shashaani, L. (1992). Gender-based differences in attitudes toward computers. *Computers and Education, 20,* 169-189.

Shashaani, L. (1994a). Socioeconomic status, parents' sex-role stereotypes, and the Gender Gap in Computing. *Journal of Research on Computing in Education, 26,* 433-451.

Shashaani, L. (1994b). Gender differences in computer experience and its influence on computer attitudes. *Journal of Educational Computing Research. 11,* 347-367.

Spradley, J. P. (1979). *The ethnographic interview.* New York: Holt, Rhinehart, and Winston.

Turkle, S., & Papert, S. (1990). Epistemological pluralism: styles and voices within the computer culture. *Signs: Journal of women in culture and society*, *16*, 128-157.

Vernon-Gerstenfeld, S. (1989). Serendipity? Are there gender differences in the adoption of computers? A case study. *Sex Roles*, *21*, 161-173.

Webb, M. E. (1994). Beginning computer-based modeling in primary schools. *Computers and Education*, *22*, 129-144.

Wilder, G., Mackie, D., & Cooper, J. (1985). Gender and computers: Two surveys of computer-related attitudes. *Sex Roles*, *13*, 215-228.

Yin, R. K. (1989). *Case study research design and methods*. Newbury Park: Sage Publications.

# Index

Page numbers followed by *t* indicate tables. *Italic* numbers indicate photographs.

# Women and Computer Based Technologies

## A Feminist Perspective

Hope Morritt

University Press of America, Inc.
Lanham • New York • Oxford

Copyright © 1997 by
**University Press of America,® Inc.**
4720 Boston Way
Lanham, Maryland 20706

12 Hid's Copse Rd.
Cummor Hill, Oxford OX2 9JJ

**Library of Congress Cataloging-in-Publication Data**

Morritt, Hope
Women and computer based technologies : a feminist perspective /
Hope Morritt.
p.  cm.
Includes bibliographical references.
1. Women--Effect of automation on. 2. Computer literacy--Sex
differences. 3. Women in education. 4. Feminist theory. I. Title.
HQ1233.M64  1997  303.48'34'082--dc21  97-1652 CIP

ISBN 0-7618-0711-X ( cloth: alk. ppr.)
ISBN 0-7618-0712-8 (pbk: alk. ppr.)